Successful People are Full of C.R.A.P:

(Courage, Resilience, Authenticity, Perseverance)

A Step-by-Step Guide to Getting it Together & Achieving Your Dreams

Rachel Luna

To my mom Carmen Santini, the wind beneath my wings. I thank and praise God every single day for bringing us together. I will never be able to thank you enough for the life you have given me.
To my daughters Isabella and Valentina, you are the reasons I wake up every morning. You will forever have my heart and soul.
To my husband, Dakar, I am blessed beyond measure. You have made my dreams come true. I love you, today, tomorrow and always.

How To Get The Most Out Of This Book

1. If ya got the e-book, print this bad mammer-jammer out and throw it in a binder or folder so you can scribble, scrabble and take notes all over the place.

2. Don't skip the questions and exercises. Take the time to <u>do the work</u>! Because really, if you're not going to do the work, why did you pick this book up in the first place?

3. Get a group of friends and start a success club. Read through the book together and support one another along the way. Be sure and let me know if you've created a group so I can send you folks some extra love.

4. Don't be afraid to reach out to me as you read through it. I'm always available at www.thetailormadelife.com or via email at info@thetailormadelife.com.

Contents

STOP! READ THE INTRO.
DO NOT PASS GO.
DO NOT SKIP AHEAD TO CHAPTER 1.

Introduction

Hello dear reader. I wanted to be deliberate in my request for you to read the intro. If you're like me, you tend to skip things like boring intros and jump right on into the "good" stuff in the chapters. Well not so fast partner! I want us to spend a few minutes together to give you some insight and share my intent for this book. I wrote this book because for years I was gripped with fear, I was following other people's dreams and ignoring my own. When things got tough, I would make excuses or quit altogether. Every day I spent ignoring my passion was another day I felt I was losing just a little piece of myself. Maybe this sounds familiar to you, and maybe it doesn't. But I suspect if you're reading this book (and it wasn't a gift from my mom) then maybe, just maybe, you feel NOW is the time to start making a change and start living the life you were born to have.

You'll get the most out of this book if you already have an idea of what is your passion or dream. If you're thinking to yourself, *'I have no freakin' clue what my dream is,'* I want to challenge you with this question: Do you really not know what you want or are you just afraid to go for it? This is a super tough question, because it really forces you to look at yourself and the decisions you've made in life to date. In fact, a lot of this book will challenge you to go deep and ask yourself some tough questions. I promise you though, if you do the work, if you answer the questions with an honest heart, you'll get a ton of knowledge, guidance and inspiration from this book.

This book is for you if:

- ✔ You have made decisions in your life under the influence of others.
- ✔ Fear has stopped you from going after the things you wanted.
- ✔ You don't wake up every day excited about your career and life as a whole.
- ✔ You feel you're slowly wasting away into a life of complacent, mundane, uneventful routine.
- ✔ Your soul hurts from lack of personal and professional fulfillment.
- ✔ You are ready for change and you'll do just about anything it takes to have the life of your dreams.

A word of caution: I am a straight talker. I am all about taking action and stretching you past your comfort zone because that is the only way you're going to get what you want. If you can't handle that, then we are not a match made in heaven and I want you to put this book back where you found it. I speak boldly because I have been exactly where you are. I have been unhappy, sad, depressed, frustrated and at my breaking point in every aspect of my life, spiritually, physically, financially and emotionally. And having been there and done that, I also know from experience that sometimes we need to hear things more than once before we take real, serious action. Admittedly, I'll be the first to tell you there really isn't much material in this book of a profound nature. What I'm sharing with you is stuff you need to hear or rehear to help you get it together and achieve your dreams. Beyond just hearing, my goal for you in this book is to get you moving into action. Stop wishing, stop hoping and start doing! That being said, I strongly encourage you to have an open mind, take the exercises seriously and do the work. It's really the only way you're going to have the life you want.

Here's what you're going to get out of this book:

- Motivation, encouragement, inspiration and no BS ways to move forward despite your fears.
- Strategies for living a more authentic life.
- Guided instruction for developing an attitude of resilience and perseverance.
- Instruction on how to create your mission statement, develop your personal brand, and a detailed outline for developing a plan to finance your dream.
- A step-by-step implementation plan to guide you as you work towards achieving your dream.
- A few good laughs and some wonderfully inspiring stories from highly successful people who are full of C.R.A.P.

If all that sounds good to you, then let's get cookin' baby. Head on over to Chapter 1 and let me show you how being full of courage, resilience, authenticity, and perseverance will change your life and help you fulfill your dreams.

ベW

Getting it together

"In the middle of difficulty lies opportunity."
- Albert Einstein

"When Are You Going To Get Your Life Together?"

In late 2003, a young 23-year-old Marine Reservist returned back to her job as an analyst in corporate America after a 7-month tour in Kuwait and Iraq. For the next year or so she would advance on schedule but never feel quite fulfilled. In the back of her mind all she could think was, *These people are getting all bent out of shape over the number of cars sold. Don't they realize people are out there fighting for their lives? Life has to be about more than just numbers on an excel spreadsheet.* Yet, she stayed because it was a comfortable job at a great company with outstanding benefits. Deep down inside, she just knew she was destined to live a more purposeful life – one that didn't rely on the accuracy of an excel spreadsheet or volume of sales.

I was that 23 year old and in May of 2005, I decided that I had had enough. I called my mom at work one day and told her I wanted to leave beautiful Southern California and come back home to the hustle and bustle of New York City to figure things out. I didn't know what I wanted, but I knew there had to be more to life than plugging numbers and formulas into a spreadsheet. She tried to persuade me to stay where I was, crying, *"C'mon Rachel. You have a great job. You have benefits. What are you going to do here in New York? You don't even have a job lined up."* You see, my mom grew up rather poor in a small town in Puerto Rico.

Her parents had grown up during the Great Depression and were raising 12 children including my mom. To all of them, the greatest thing you could do was go to college, get a good job with good benefits and if you were lucky, a nice pension plan. That's what my mom was raised to believe, and that's what she wanted for me. It took a bit of convincing on my part, but my mother finally relented and agreed I could stay with her while I got myself together. As soon as I hung up the phone I purchased a one-way ticket to JFK, made a call to the Marine Corps recruiter near my mom's apartment and asked if they would consider bringing me on board as a temporary recruiter. He enthusiastically replied, "Hell yes!" and armed with all the gumption I had, I marched into my boss' office and gave him my letter of resignation. My apartment was packed two weeks later and I was on my way home to live the life of my dreams. Or so I thought…

Things didn't quite fall into place as smoothly as I had thought they would. The Marine recruiter had spoken too soon and as it turned out, they were not interested in bringing a Sergeant (my rank at the time) on board because with my salary they could bring in three Marines of lesser rank. In military recruiting it's all about the numbers and three bodies doing the work is much more desirable than one. So there I was, 25 years old, unemployed and living in my mom's home. I was definitely NOT living the life of my dreams. Thankfully my sister made a few calls on my behalf and I ended up working as an administrative coordinator at Goldman Sachs. The salary was peanuts compared to what I had been making at my old job, but the work actually wasn't so bad. I enjoyed the tasks of scheduling, processing expense reports, and supervising a team of other administrative assistants – and best of all, I got to watch TV on the job. There was a huge flat screen right in front of my desk that showed all the great morning shows and news programs. I probably would have stayed there forever had it not been for my mother's routine wake up call.

"Rachel, wake up. It's time to go to work. When are you going to get your life together? You need to figure things out. And hurry up or you're going to be late."
Yes, that is really how she woke me up every single day for the 6 months I spent in her house "figuring things out." It's now a running joke, but for those 6 months it was my reality. Coasting through life wasn't such a bad gig, but I kept feeling as though life was passing me by. Sure, I worked in a super easy job, conveniently located right next to one of my favorite NYC attractions, the South Street Seaport, and yes, on more than one occasion I'd indulge in a lunchtime frozen margarita with the girls, but something was missing. I mean, I was supposed to be a famous actress by now. What the heck was I doing answering phones and watching MSNBC all day? This was NOT my life.

And then I got my big break! It was a beautiful Monday afternoon when I got a phone call from a friend in Los Angeles. He had a bit part for me in a pilot series that could possibly turn into a recurring role, but I'd need to be back in LA by Wednesday. Never afraid of taking a risk, I walked into my boss's office and asked for a leave of absence. She wasn't thrilled but I didn't care, I wasn't really planning on coming back anyway. I bought a one-way ticket back to LA, went home, packed all my stuff and boarded a plane the very next morning. My mom thought I was crazy and I'm pretty sure she spent the entire night praying for my sanity, but I made it just in time to shoot the pilot. Unfortunately, the show was cancelled and they even cut the season short with four episodes left unaired. Oh and my bit part, turned out to be a super, itty, bitty part. You might be able to catch me if you watch it in slow motion. Some big break, huh? So there I was, back in LA, no job and living with my dear friend and favorite roomie, Emely. But hey, at least I was out of my mom's house and back on my own. This time I was going to find my true passion come hell or high water. For the next six months I waited tables, took acting classes and went on a few auditions. I did enough work to earn my SAG (Screen Actor's Guild) card and even scored a small part on JAG as a stunt boxer. That was probably the highlight of my acting career. Again, you'd have to watch the episode in slo-mo to catch a glimpse of me. All in all, pursuing an acting career was quite the learning experience. I discovered I had some serious stage fright. Every time I auditioned I'd blank out and couldn't tap into my fountain of emotion. I'd do great rehearsing my monologues at home, I could even cry on demand, but when it came for the moment of truth, I'd choke. Not a good fit for a wannabe actress. I also learned that I have a terrible memory. With two strikes against me, this acting business didn't look like it was going to pan out. The third and final strike for my acting career was the realization that I just didn't want it bad enough. I enjoyed acting classes and doing small plays but I really didn't enjoy working as a waitress and struggling until I made it big. In retrospect, I just wasn't passionate about the field of acting. I wasn't willing to do whatever it might take to make it happen. It was confirmed, I was not going to be the next J. Lo. I needed to come up with a back up plan and quick.

And just like that, I caught another break. The Marine Corps offered to bring me back on active duty to fill a spot down in Camp Pendleton. Now the Marine Corps, that was a job I loved. I was passionate about being a leader and mentoring others. While working on Camp Pendleton an opportunity opened up for me to work at the Landstuhl Regional Medical Center in Landstuhl, Germany as a patient liaison to wounded warriors. It was there that I finally discovered my passion and purpose for helping others. With the help of a life coach, I identified my strengths, weaknesses and gifts and discovered that I would thrive as a coach to others. I had already spent 8 years motivating and encouraging others in the Marine Corps and life coaching seemed like the perfect next step. I enrolled in a certification program at the International Coach Academy and the rest is history.

It wasn't always an easy ride. There were many bumps in the road, along with a plethora of comments from the peanut gallery. I had figured out what I wanted to do with my life *and* had actually gotten my mom on board, only to have other jokers tell me things like, *"Life coach? Is that a real job? Why don't you just stick with a GS (government service) job? You've already put so much time into the Marine Corps; why would you want to start over? It's not like you're fresh out of college..."* And on and on. The questions and negative comments were deafening, (again not from my mom, she'll want you to know she has been and always will be supportive of my dreams). But everyone one sure did have an opinion about my life. Go figure. People always have something to say about your life. But I didn't have time to waste listening to their negativity. Yes, in the heat of the moment, when they were questioning my ambitions or down-talking my plans, it hurt. There were many times I felt discouraged and even fearful about my future. Heck, there were plenty of days I considered quitting before really giving it a real start. But after some positive self-talk, I reminded myself that I had already spent too much time doing what other people wanted me to do. It wasn't about proving them wrong or showing them what I was capable of achieving. It was about following my heart. I needed to follow the career path that really made my heart sing – and coaching was it.

Working as a life and business coach is nothing like work for me. It feels more like an amazing privilege. Aside from my family, nothing gives me greater joy than helping someone move forward, follow their dreams and achieve success. My hope for you is that this book will help *you* move forward, follow your dreams and become the most successful person you can be. I wanted to share a bit of my story with you for two reasons: 1) so you can get to know a little about me, since we'll be spending some time together, and 2) to reassure you that you are not alone. We've all experienced some variation of my story above. There may be someone pressuring you to pursue a career path you're just not ready to pursue, you may have someone telling you that you're past your prime, or maybe you have someone telling you you're completely off your rocker. Perhaps you're telling yourself those things. Whatever your scenario is, I want you to take a minute right now to silence those voices.

Close your eyes, clear out all the background noise and tell yourself this;

Self, in this very moment, I purpose my life to achieve my dream. I silence the voices of doubt and I fill my life, my spirit and my surroundings with positivity and prosperity.

If you've never taken a moment to meditate before, then this will probably feel odd. Don't worry, just go with it. Change is uncomfortable, so if you feel uncomfy, you're doing it right!

"Lord, Give Me A Sign!"

Life would be so much simpler if we were all born with a lil' note from the big "man" (or woman) upstairs, attached on our umbilical cords, telling us the meaning of life and what we're supposed to do with it. There'd be no room for error. We could simply take our assignment and run with it. But alas, we're born buck-naked. So we go through life in pursuit of our "purpose." This whole idea of "life purpose" means a lot of different things to different people. Since this is a book about success, we're going to assume your life's purpose is to follow your dream. We're also going to assume that because you're reading this book, you've already decided that you've got to pursue your dream or die trying. Okay, maybe you won't go as far as to die trying, but you'll come pretty darn close.

"Dream A Little Dream"

What the heck do you do if you have no idea what your dream is and yet, you're life's purpose is to follow your dream? I know there's at least one person reading this book who believes they don't have a dream. I think that's horse poop. We have all had a dream at least once in our lives. Heck, as kids we had all kinds of wild dreams. We wanted to be cowboys, doctors, actors, firefighters, moms, wives, Harvard graduates, millionaires, billionaires, and everything in between. When I was a little girl, I wanted to be an actress. I already told you about my failed attempt to make it big in Hollywood, but at least by trying, I discovered what I didn't want. I didn't want to go on audition after audition and subject myself to the scrutiny of producers and directors; I just wanted to be rich and famous. I was really attracted to the glitz and glam portrayed by Hollywood – the fancy parties, the red carpet and gorgeous gowns, and of course the over-the-top, lavish lifestyle. But as I've evolved I have also learned that I probably wouldn't enjoy the paparazzi and tabloids all up in my Kool-Aid, reporting on my every move. Nope, I value my privacy and enjoy the fact that I can walk into a store unnoticed. Now the part about wanting to be rich, well, that's still on my agenda, but I remind you, riches are more than just financial. But I digress. The point is, we've all dreamt of something but have allowed life, circumstance and the negativity of others or our own fear stand in our way. We'll talk more about the negativity of others and fear in later chapters, but for now let's try and figure out your dream. If you know your dream, then you can pass go and collect $200 over in the section titled "The best place to start is at the end." If not, here are three strategies that will help you get one step closer to figuring out your dream.

#1. Question yourself every day. Ask yourself, what do I really want? You might want to get a pretty journal or notebook so you can write down the answers to this question. Review your answers carefully and meditate on them. Give yourself permission to think BIG. Identifying your dream is not the same as identifying a job path. A job path is a means to an end. A dream path is a road to fulfillment. What do you *really* want?

#2. *Use your imagination.* Many people live unfulfilled lives because they've stopped using their imagination and thinking of the possibilities. Think out of the box; let your imagination run wild. What brings you joy? If you could do anything at all, what would you do? In that pretty little notebook or journal we mentioned, make a list of all the things you love or have an interest in. If you enjoy taking pictures, why not try selling some of your photos as stock art? Do you love watching cooking shows on TV? Why not start a blog about your favorite recipes? Have you always enjoyed arts and crafts? Consider opening an Etsy store and putting your love out into the world. The possibilities are endless If you allow yourself to be open and let your imagination run wild.

#3. *Give yourself permission.* This is probably the most powerful strategy of all for identifying your dream. As you begin to answer the questions in your notebook or create your list of loves, a lot of doubt, fear, and negative self-talk will creep in. During those times, you'll need to give yourself permission to continue to think big and search without rest for your dream. It's okay to want more than what you have now. It's okay to want to follow an untraditional path. It's okay to change careers even though you've been in your industry for 15 years. None of that matters. The only thing that matters is that you stay true to yourself and give yourself permission to follow your true dream.

The process to identify your dreams and passions is one that can take extensive work and research. Don't be discouraged if it doesn't happen overnight. Just keep plugging away until you find the thing that takes your breath away and makes your heart beat. You'll know you found it, because you'll feel the butterflies and an immense sense of excitement. Now – go find your dream!

"The Best Place To Start Is At The End."

One of the first exercises I have clients do is write a letter to themselves. In this letter they answer these questions:
What does your end result look like?

When all is said and done, what does your dream life look like?

Many times they've never even considered these questions. They may even counter back, *"Wait. What? What does my future look like? I don't know. I guess I never thought about it."* Rightly so, these questions have never been posed because many people are living on autopilot. Just going with the flow and letting their dreams blow away in the wind. Well no more I tell you! **No más!** If you haven't thought about what your end result looks like, now is the time. How else will you know how to your destination if you have no clue of where you want to go? If you don't have a clear vision of what your end result looks like but know that being financially independent is an integral part of that vision, then it is of even greater importance that you take the time to start focusing in on your desired end result. Only then can you carefully devise a plan that will take you where you need and want to be.

"Q & A With Your Soul"

Let's go back to school and do a little fill in the blank activity. My dream is to be a self made/owned SFx MUA .

Congratulations! You are now one step closer towards achieving your dream – because those who write down their goals and desires are much more likely to achieve them than those who don't. But we're just getting started. In order to really make your mark and achieve the success you desire, you need to have a question and answer session with your soul. The following questions are vital to your success:

Why is this your dream?

Have you done the research to find out what it will take to get there?

Are you passionate about your dream?

Are you in *love* with your dream?

What will your life be like if you don't achieve your dream?

Think about these questions for a few minutes. Now that you've had a moment to think and reflect on these questions, let's take a closer look. Why is this your dream? I'm sorry to be the one to tell you this, but if you don't know your "why" there's a pretty good chance you won't achieve your dream. It's time for what my clients and I call, "A Hard Truth with Rachel" moment. The hard truth is, knowing your "why" is likely to be the only thing that will get you through the tough times. If you don't know or don't take the time to figure out your "why" then I regret to inform you, you're headed up the creek and there isn't a paddle in sight. Right now, take some time and think about why the dream you wrote above is so important to you.

The next discussion question forces you to assess how much you really know about your dream. After all, before someone invests their money into a stock, a company or what-have-you, they do a bit of research to see what their return on the investment will be. The same should be true with your career/dream/goal or life path. If you don't know all the ins and outs of your dream, then it's time to go to school. So I'll ask you again:

Have you done the research to find out what it will take to help you achieve your dream? Circle YES or NO.

If you circled NO, then let's take action right now! Get out a pen and list 3 things you need to research or learn about your dream:

_____

_____

_____

Next, set a deadline to get the research done. Deadline:

_____

This exercise will help you get a very clear understanding of what you need to know to position yourself for success. Yes, there have been people who have made it by chance, who have stumbled into their dream life just by walking down the street, but those people are the minority.

Do your due diligence! I used to tell people, "I'm a jack of all trades, a master of none." It's great to be a jack-of-all-trades because then you know a little bit about a lot of things, but it's even better to be a master in your field. If you want success, you need people to take you seriously, and the only way that will happen is if you know what the heck you're talking about!

The next couple of questions I asked you to think about in the beginning of this section, go hand in hand. Are you passionate about your dream? Are you in love with it? I purposefully use the words passionate and love. When you are on the road to success, it gets bumpy. Boy, does it get bumpy. Some days it feels like you're hitting every red light, and each corner is a no-crossing zone. It can get down-right depressing and may even make you feel like turning around and calling it quits. But if you are passionate and in love with your dream, then you can easily convert those red lights and no-crossing zones into minor detours and continue on your way. This is why I encourage you to pursue the dream that you are in love with and most passionate about. When you hit the road-

You know you are on the road to success if you would do your job, and not be paid for it. – *Oprah Winfrey*

blocks, come back to this section and ask yourself these questions all over again. Oprah Winfrey once said, "*You know you are on the road to success if you would do your job, and not be paid for it.*" I share that quote with you because THAT is true love. When you remember the love and passion you have for your dream, it will be that much easier to get you through the bumpy times.

Finally, the questions I encourage you to really consider are what will your life be like if you don't achieve your dream? Would you be happy living your life without ever having achieved or even attempted your dream? I'm going to guess not, but that's up to you to decide.

"Haters Are Gonna Hate"

Roadblocks and stop signs aside, along the way you'll encounter people I like to call *haters*. These are people who tell you things like: you're too young, you're too old, you're dreaming too much, you're seeking the impossible, it's never gonna happen, just forget about it, etc. *Haters* can be one of two things: success kryptonite or success ammo. It depends on your perspective. If you choose to listen to these people and let them get into your psyche, then you might as well stop reading this book right now. Put It down and rologate yourself to a life of what-ifs and shoulda, coulda, woulda's. Because, while it's certainly easy for me to sit here and tell you to ignore them, the reality is, once people get into your head, it's hard to get them out. Your own doubts and fears show up for the pity party, insecurities set in and you start to sink down into a dark world of limiting beliefs.

On the other hand, if you choose to hear these people and use their words as motivation to prove them wrong, then you're in for the ride of your life. A dear friend of mine, Eric

Haters = lighter fluid.

Anthony Johnson, CEO of Javaboi Industries says, "*Haters = lighter fluid.*" Can I get an amen?

The bottom line is this: *Haters are gonna hate.* There's no escape. As my friend Leslie recently posted on her Facebook wall, "*Nowadays, everybody got something to say about your life but ain't doin' nothing with they own.*" Haters especially, always have something to say when people around them are doing well and getting themselves on the path to success. And let me tell you, my friend, I've had my fair share of haters. My first hater memory goes all the way back to my junior year at St. Vincent Ferrer High School (an all girls school, mind you). I had a meeting with the guidance counselor, who shall remain nameless (and no, she doesn't work there anymore) to discuss my senior year schedule. As we were chatting, I began to tell her of my plan to take Advanced Placement English. She gave me this incredulous look and said, "*You have no business taking AP English. You're an average student with average grades. If you take AP you'll just fail it.*" No bull, this is what my "guidance" counselor told me! Okay, so she did have a point – I wasn't doing so hot in a lot of my classes, particularly math. But I was doing great in English. It was my favorite subject. Who the heck did she think she was? How dare she tell me I was going to fail? I had to fight back tears as I walked out of her office, but, let me tell you, that chic ignited a fire inside of me like none other. I made a beeline for Miss Rosier, my English teacher, who was also the AP English teacher at the time, and asked her if she thought I'd make it. She confirmed what I knew all along; I was an excellent English student and I'd do great in the AP class. Thank you, dear, sweet, kind and gentle Miss Rosier, wherever you are!

I ended up transferring out of St. Vincent Ferrer my senior year for other reasons (read: I was cutting class and wasting my potential) and started anew at Lancaster Mennonite High School in Lancaster, Pennsylvania. I was accepted to their AP English class where I did great, just as I knew I would. Incidentally, I graduated my senior year with a 3.8 G.P.A. Take that, Miss Know-it-all, guidance counselor!

At the end of the day, it's up to you to decide how the haters will affect your life. Are you going to follow their lead and talk your life away, or are you going to follow your dreams and let them take notes? I say grab your ammo and lighter fluid and go start a fire!

"The Power Of Planning"

Most people think that 'figuring it out' is the challenge, but the real battle begins when you take the steps to make a dream a reality. So how do you do it? How do you take the first step? Check this: your dream isn't just some random gig. This is your *dream*. Do you want to leave your dream to chance? No. Heck, no, foolio! You want to take a few minutes to sharpen your crayons and get ready to color. It's time to get a plan together. You don't need a 300-page business plan, nor do you have to follow every little detail outlined in the plan. That's probably impossible to do anyway, because life is constantly changing. What I'm saying is, if you have a plan, you'll be that much more ahead of the game. Know what you want, make a plan to get there, and then follow your plan with passion. In chapter 10, we'll go into the nuts and bolts of putting your plan together, but for now, put the seed in your mind that you'll be growing a plan.

"Preparing For Success"

Alright, you've identified your dream, you're ready to pursue it, you've had a good heart-to-heart with your soul, decided to use the *Haters* as success ammo, and you've planted a seed to start planning your path to success. You've done a lot! Congratulate yourself for taking these very essential first steps. But the pot of success soup is just starting to simmer. The next thing you have to do is prepare yourself for success. A lot of us want to be successful but as we get close and eventually get there, we don't know what to do with ourselves because we didn't take the time to get ready mentally as well as emotionally. There are many ways you can prepare yourself, but I want to highlight the top 5 steps:

Prep Step #1 Visualize:

Think about the success you want and visualize your life as already having achieved it. When you visualize your world, as you want it to be, something in your subconscious kicks into overdrive and forces you to go after your dreams with even more vigor. You might not even realize it's happening, but your subconscious is hard at work laying the foundation for that road to success.

Let's try a quick visualization exercise. Say your dream is to be a best-selling author. Close your eyes, envision what your book jacket looks like, and visualize your name at the top of the New York Times Best-Sellers List. Imagine your signature at the end of emails reading "New York Times Best Selling Author." The possibilities are endless. Let your imagination run wild as you see yourself becoming the person you've always dreamed of being. This exercise is powerful, so do it!

Prep Step #2: Fake it 'til you make it:

Now that you've put a picture in your mind of what you living your dream looks like, start to walk in those shoes. When people ask you what you do, confidently say, *"I'm a writer," "I'm an actress," "I own my own business,"* etc. Whatever you want your life to be, you just have to fake it until you make it. Before I'd written even one word of this book I was walking around town telling people, *"I'm a writer."* Before I landed my first speaking gig, my signature block said Rachel Luna, Speaker. You get the gist.

If you want to be successful, you have to act successful. Try it right now with this fun fill in the blank activity. I'm asking you, *"Reader, what's your dream?"* You reply, *"I'm a _____."* Now say it out loud and with confidence! You are a _____! I know it, you know it, now let's make sure the world knows it!

Prep Step #3: Prepare to be disappointed:

I can't tell you how many times my clients have used some variation of the expression, *"If I don't expect much then I won't be disappointed."* Whenever I hear this I want to shake them. Of course you should expect big things for yourself. You should be expecting to succeed each and every day. But yes, you should also prepare for disappointment. Breaking news: disappointments are part of life. If you have high expectations, then maybe you have a higher risk of disappointment, but you also have a greater risk of success!

I'm not saying you should walk around thinking, *"I'm going to fail."* What I *am* saying is that you should be

One's best success comes after one's greatest disappointments.
– *Henry Ward Beecher*

prepared to *deal with* disappointment and have a plan in place for the unlikely event. For example, if your dream is to be an actor, then you know right from the jump you'll be turned down for roles. After all, not every actor can land every role. So prepare yourself emotionally to deal with that experience and remember it's okay to be disappointed – but don't be discouraged. The other thing you need to keep in mind is that you are not being rejected personally. It wasn't the right time or the right opportunity for you at that moment. It doesn't make you less special, nor does it mean your dream is dead. It just means you may have to take a few steps back and find another approach. In the words of Henry Ward Beecher, *"One's best success comes after one's greatest disappointments."*

Prep Step #4: Focus on fitness:

How many times have you said to yourself, *"I'll start eating better and exercising on Monday?"* Well, guess what, friend? It's Monday and the time is now. It takes a tremendous amount of stamina and energy to pursue your dream, day after day, with enthusiasm and zest. In order to achieve success you must have focused mental clarity. The best way to ensure this happens is to take care of yourself. Limit your intake of sugar, fatty foods, caffeine and alcohol. Now don't get me wrong, I Love (with a capital L), Love Krispy Kreme®, Dunkin' Donuts®, and of course the ever-tasty Starbucks Iced Caramel Macchiato® with whipped cream just as much as the next person, but these foods shouldn't be staples, they're luxuries. I'm not going to go on and lecture you about becoming an ultra fitness buff, but we all know that exercise is a great stress reliever. In fact, researchers at Duke University concluded that regular exercise has antidepressant properties – perfect to help you get over a disappointment swiftly and with ease. Even going for a simple, brisk walk releases wonderful endorphins that can aid in creativity. So keep an eye on your food intake and start walking (or running if you're really motivated)! Oh, and if you're one of those people who haven't yet identified your dream, then you should definitely put this prep step into practice. I get some of my best ideas when I'm in motion and in Chapter 11, you'll read an interview I conducted with a dear friend of mine who has become a huge success in the fitness industry. She's taking care of herself, living her dream and making some serious dinero too. I'm just sayin', focusing on fitness really does pay off.

Prep Step #5: Expect success:

This may sound a bit contrary to step 3 where I tell you to prepare for disappointment, but the bottom line is this - if you want to be successful, you have to *expect* to be successful. That's that. Nothing fancy, no special formula. Have an attitude of expectation. *"When you expect success, your mind focuses on success."* – Anonymous.

**"When you expect success,
your mind focuses on success."**
– Anonymous.

Let's Wrap It Up

Great job "getting it together" and making it through chapter 1. We've covered a lot of information, so let's recap the highlights.

- ✔ Change is uncomfortable, so if you feel uncomfy, you're doing it right!

- ✔ Let the *Haters* be your success ammo.

- ✔ Know what you want, make a plan to get there, and then follow that plan with passion.

- ✔ Have a regular Q& A Session with your soul to get you through the bumpy roads.

- ✔ Utilize the Prep Steps for Success:

  1. Visualize
  2. Fake it 'til you make it
  3. Prepare for disappointment
  4. Focus on fitness
  5. Expect success

Notes:

_____
_____
_____
_____
_____
_____

Now let's move onto Chapter 2. Turn the page if you have the courage. Actually, you better turn the page and keep reading even if you don't have courage, because I'm going to show you how living courageously leads to success. Go on, turn the page.

Courage Is Highly Underrated

"Fear and courage are brothers."

– Proverb

"Courage vs. Fear"

In Chapter One, I promised to show you how living courageously leads to success. To do this, you must first have a clear understanding of the word "courage." Courage is, "the quality of mind or spirit that enables a person to face difficulty, danger, pain, etc., without fear"[1] . Thesaurus.com lists courage as a synonym for fearlessness. Is that how you define courage? Do you really think people who have engaged in courageous acts did so absent of fear? I don't think so – let's dig a bit further.

"Courage, Redefined"

All of us are afraid of *something*. To go around living each day without fear is quite a challenge, probably even close to impossible. Enter my definition of courage: "the ability to face a difficult moment *despite* fear." Courage is moving forward even though you are scared. Am I telling you not to conquer your fears? No, of course you should work on conquering your fears. But overcoming them isn't a task achieved overnight. This is why being courageous – as I define it – is so important. On your journey to success, you're going to face challenges that scare you and put you out of your comfort zone. You simply can't let precious opportunities pass you by while you're working on getting over your

---

1   www.dictionary.com/courage

fear. You've got to take advantage of every chance you get, despite it!

"Confidence, Cojones & Doggone Ovaries"

In boot camp I had a drill instructor named, Sergeant Phillips, who would always scream, *"Reach down deep and grab your doggone ovaries,"* whenever anyone was struggling with a particular task. At the time, I hated her because she was the toughest on us. The very sound of her voice would piss me off and I'd push myself even harder just so sho'd shut the hell up. But there was one pivotal moment during a night fire exercise when she wasn't around, but her words still haunted me. The purpose of this exercise was to simulate being on the battlefield at night catching fire (catching fire means people shooting at you). The challenge was to low crawl the distance of the course with our weapon and a few ammunition boxes. These boxes were freaking heavy. Between our team of four, we had two small boxes that weighed about thirty pounds each and two larger boxes that weighed about sixty pounds each. As the first shot was fired signifying the start of the event I grabbed my small box and hit the deck. Pushing my way through the course I felt a rush of adrenaline. Although I knew it was fake, it felt so real. I felt the urgency of the situation. How would I respond if this were a real war? Is this what the sky would look like, all lit up with heavy artillery? It reminded me of the Macy's fireworks display. Right in that moment, confidence I had never known before rushed through me and I took off like Superwoman. I was ahead of a few of my teammates who had been partnered up to push the sixty pound box but I could hear them arguing on how they were going to make it across. Again, the point of the exercise was to make sure you and your possessions crossed, so you couldn't just leave your ammo box and save yourself. A box full of ammunition is a treasure for the enemy. I kept pressing on, trudging through the sand box course, dropped my box at the finish line and looked back to see my teammates struggling. They still had more than half the course to finish. That's when the months of listening to Sergeant Phillips kicked in and I found my doggone ovaries. I ran back into the course to get my friends. In the background I could hear my drill instructors yelling at me, *"Rodriguez, what the hell are you doing?"* (Rodriguez is my maiden name). I didn't take the time to answer them, I just knew that my friends needed help and Marines don't leave Marines behind. Yes, I know, that sounds so very dramatic, but I was a very impressionable 19 year old with a highly active imagination. This was war, damn it! I threw myself on the deck and told the one girl who was struggling most to just go ahead. Then I began shouting orders at my other friend to push on my count. Together she and I crossed the line and the team passed the test. A week or so later at graduation the commander for 4th Battalion, Lieutenant Colonel Frasier Darling, came up to me and said, *"Rodriguez, was that you that went back into the course during night fire?"* *"Yes ma'am, that was, ma'am,"* I replied, actually scared she was going to reprimand me right there on graduation day. *"Well done, Rodriguez. You're the kind of Marine I want to go to war with."* I still get the chills when I think of

"the way you practice is the way you perform."

that defining moment in my life. It was not a real war. It was nothing like a real war. But all my life, I've lived by the motto *"the way you practice is the way you perform."* In that moment, I had given that practice my all. I did end up going to war several years later. Thankfully, I never had to come under direct fire, but there were many times we had to don our gas masks or take cover in bunkers because of air strikes and I knew that if anything went down, I had some doggone ovaries and I could handle it. As a disclaimer, I want to stress that none of my actions when I did get deployed were anything that could be associated with the real bravery it takes to survive in combat. There are *real* heroes out there, men and women, who have been on the front lines taking fire night after night. Those are the bravest of the brave. But I shared this little story of my personal experience to show you that we can each be brave and courageous in our day-to-day lives. Whether it's a simulated battlefield or in a boardroom, successful people make their mark by walking with courage, confidence, cojones and doggone ovaries every step of the way.

"Pushing Past The F-word"

We've covered the difference between courage and fear and why having courage, confidence and doggone ovaries are essential to your success. Now let's give fear a little more attention. Fear is a nasty little four-letter word. Yet for some reason, people don't seem to have a problem saying or living with it. Why not? Because we've become desensitized. We accept fear as part of the norm, because well, it is – but it shouldn't be.

In a perfect world, we'd be able to snap our fingers and banish the things we're afraid of. Alas, we're mere mortals with a choice to make: brave our fears or succumb to them. What if, for a moment, we consider a third option? What if rather than either giving into or conquering it, we simply chose to push past the fear? This doesn't mean pretending we don't feel or experience it; rather, we embody courage and move forward despite the f-word. There are many ways to do this, and the key is to find what works for you. There is no one right way to do anything, just the right way that works for you in the moment. That's how my friend, who has an extreme fear of flying, approaches traveling. Each trip is an opportunity to figure out a way to make flying work for her.

My dear friend loves to travel, but hates to fly. Days leading up to a trip, she gets nervous, doesn't sleep well, has mini panic attacks and the list goes on. The bottom line is that she's a hot mess before a trip. Okay, I confess, the friend is me. Walking the tarmac is like walking the plank. My palms are sweaty, I'm hyperventilating and all I can think is, *Please don't let me die, please don't let me die.* Once in my seat, I explain to the flight attendant how terrified I am and ask for a bottle of vodka before we take off to help calm my nerves. This is usually brought to me super-fast and free of charge. Ahhh, the perks of being afraid to fly the friendly skies.

It's an ordeal every time I get on a plane. But I love to travel, so I have to fly to get to where I really want to be. I share this with you to paint a picture: we all have some deep-rooted fear that could suck the joy out of life and prevent us from doing the things we love – if we let it. Each time I get on a plane, I'm not without trepidation – quite the contrary – but I do my best to walk with courage so I can enjoy the experience of travel. That's what pushing past the f-word is all about. My story really isn't unique. There are even professional entertainers who have stage fright. The great Barbara Streisand suffered from stage fright for many years. She even quit doing live performances for quite some time because of this fear. Finally she decided she wasn't going to let that stop her from performing live any more and she went on to give amazing concerts all over the world. She pushed past it, and you can, too!

"Courage By Default"

What if, despite your best efforts, your fear continues to plague you? That's when I like to practice a little technique I call "courage by default." Here's how it works: you identify the fear or obstacle holding you back and then you craft a way to get to your goal. You can delegate someone to take on the challenge for you, you can ignore your fear by implementing distraction techniques, or you can use those feelings as fuel to get you through the obstacle.

A client of mine, Lydia,* recently expressed a fear of cold calling people to gain support for an upcoming project. Among her concerns were fear of rejection coupled

*Names have been changed

with the potential for her to muddle her words, not be taken seriously, and come across as unintelligent. In reality, her project was solid. She's incredibly talented and intelligent. Her fears were holding her back from realizing a really fabulous venture.

As we began to discuss the ramifications, the truth became clear very quickly: the only way she was going to be able to forge ahead was by practicing *courage by default* and delegating the task. She hired a friend to work with her for a week and paid her $100 to make the calls. The result: Lydia's "assistant" for the week brought on 10 supporters and a few unexpected business collaboration opportunities. While Lydia didn't overcome her fear of cold calling, she was still able to do the courageous thing and ask for help, which then enabled her to achieve her goal.

The principle of *courage by default* can be applied to just about any situation. You just have to remember the 3 steps: 1. Delegate 2. Distract. 3. Fuel. Are you ready to go deeper? Let's talk about your fears. What are you most afraid of when it comes to your dream? Are you afraid of failing? Are you afraid of succeeding? Are you afraid of the work it'll take to get you there? Scared your family and friends will laugh at you? Worried people won't take you seriously? Nervous you won't make enough money if you go for it? These are just a few questions to help you get to the root of your fears. I know once you take a really good look deep inside your soul, you'll know exactly what scares you about moving forward and fulfilling your dream. List the 3 deepest fears holding you back from going after your dream:

1. _____.

2. _____.

3. _____.

Can you apply any of the *courage by default* principles to your fears? Give it a try. If all else fails, I *know* using your fears as fuel works if you work it. Now go on friend, work it!

"Courage Case Studies"

Embarking on a new venture, particularly one that involves the entrepreneurial spirit is risky business. The following are three cases studies of 3 entrepreneurs who took big risks to follow their passions. I chose these particular stories because they really took a chance on themselves. They went against the grain, against all odds, despite naysayers in their lives and followed their dreams. Do you have the courage to go for it like these people did? Check out their stories.

Lauren Luke, 28
makeup entrepreneur and YouTube sensation

Luke has parlayed her love of cosmetics into her own product line at Sephora, "By Lauren Luke," a book titled Looks by Lauren Luke *and she even has a videogame, "Supermodel Makeover by Lauren Luke." In her words, "I was working at a local taxi office taking bookings on the phone. I knew I wasn't going anywhere, so I started selling makeup full-time online. I put myself on YouTube knowing I didn't look like a model, but I didn't care."*

I stumbled onto Lauren Luke's YouTube page while trying to find makeup tutorials for my wedding day. When I found her she was just starting to create her own makeup line and I had no idea she was on her road to make-up stardom. We'll take a closer look at her story and how she got there after we learn about Tim Westergren and Heather B. Armstrong.

Tim Westergren, 44
founder of Pandora Radio

Tim Westergren was a man with a mission. He gave 348 pitches to get support for his company and boy, did that pay off! But it wasn't an easy climb to the top. Here's what Tim had to say about his big risk with Pandora Radio: "In the winter of 2001, Pandora was out of money. We had a choice: cut our losses and throw in the towel or find a way to keep going. We decided to keep the company alive and start deferring salaries. Ultimately, over 50 people deferred almost $1.5 million over the course of two years (a practice that is illegal in California). When we were finally rescued by an investment in 2004, I had maxed-out 11 credit cards." Pandora made $1.6 million in the second quarter of its 2011 fiscal year and $1 million in the third quarter.[1]

If you were in Tim's position would you have maxed out 11 credit cards? Would you have asked employees to defer their paychecks with no real guarantee? If you were an employee at Pandora, would you have given up your paycheck? These people had more than courage, they had passion. They believed in their mission, their product and themselves. Given that I don't believe in debt, I can't say I personally would have maxed out 11 credit cards, but Tim Westergren's courage inspires me. Learning about his determination and will to succeed motivate me to keep dreaming big. What about you? Can you envision yourself following your passion at all costs? Speaking of all costs, Heather B. Armstrong lost her job as a result of following her passion. But through adversity comes triumph: Armstrong landed on her feet and has never been better. Here's her story in a nutshell.

Heather B. Armstrong Founder of Dooce.com, a website about motherhood.

Armstrong began her site in 2001, like many other bloggers, as an outlet to talk about her life. Fast-forward 8 years later, Forbes named Armstrong among 30 honorees on its list of "The Most Influential Women In Media" for 2009. Heather stated, "I never really intended to make money with it. My husband found out the number of readers and realized that if we got advertising, it could support the family. I was very hesitant to do it. I knew that there was going to be a huge backlash in terms of readers thinking that this would change the tone or affect the irreverence that I use in my writing. [Finally] I said, "let's do it"-- and it's been a huge success."[1]

What's not mentioned in this nutshell of Heather's story is how she was fired from her day-job as a result of things she had written on her blog. That's crazy, right? These three people took big chances on themselves despite trepidation, insecurities, and self-doubt. If they can overcome debt, single parenting and job loss, what's stopping you?

"A Closer Look"

Let's take a more in-depth look at Lauren Luke. After having a baby at age 16, Luke recognized early on that her greatest desire was to provide a better life for her son. Her love for art and cosmetics, coupled with her desire to have a more abundant life, led Luke to start a small cosmetic business on eBay. In her own words, Luke describes her feelings on making the initial investment. *"I can remember how* hard it was to part with my savings and I wondered if the risk was worth it. I believed in what I was doing but there is also a fear in the back of your mind that you are risking everything for nothing."[2]

Does that sound familiar? Have you felt the way Lauren felt as she was considering making that initial investment? Is there a business or career path you have thought about pursuing but feared the risk was too great? You need to remember this moment and drill into your brain the concept that "*you will not achieve success without taking a chance.*" Today, *By Lauren Luke* Cosmetics are sold in over 100 Sephora Cosmetics chain stores across Canada and the U.S., and she is the author of a book titled *Looks by Lauren Luke*. She also has her own Nintendo DS Game *Supermodel Makeover*. That's the power of courage! Need I say more?

"A Note On Courage And Money"

Responsibilities and obligations are aspects of life that can make it difficult, and at times, very scary to take a step in a new direction, make the leap of faith to transition into a new career, or venture out to start your own business. Don't let your responsibilities deter you from following your dreams. That's not to say go quit your job on a whim with only $10 to your name or take out a huge business loan you can't afford – *please don't do that.* It would be extremely risky, create a lot of pressure and ultimately would not be the most intelligent move. In order to successfully make the transition, you'll need to assess your financial situation and budget for your success. Later in the book, we'll talk about the relevance between money and success, and I'll even give you the framework for funding your future. But for now, work on

2   www.laurenluke.com/my_story

building a financial cushion that will allow you to continue to pay your bills and cover your basic needs so you can really go for it and take the risk with financial peace of mind.

"Be Courageous. Be Exceptional. Have No Regret."

The worst feeling you can experience is waking up one day feeling as though you missed your chance and wasted your life. Don't be mediocre, strive to do and be your best every single day – be exceptional. Therefore, I challenge you to live courageously and take risks because once you start moving past your fears, your success factor soars exponentially. And if all else fails, there's always *courage by default*.

"The Year In Review"

Mark Twain said, *"Twenty years from now, you will be more disappointed by the things that you didn't do than by the ones you did do."* I don't know about you, but at the ripe "old" age of 31, I already feel disappointment by many of the things I didn't do. I'd hate to think I'll be adding more disappointment over the next twenty years. The only way to avoid that is to go out and do it all! Go and take the risks. Get up and make a change in your life today, not tomorrow. Even consider your life in just this past year. Are you disappointed by any of the things you did or didn't do this year? Let's examine the last 12 months of your life and give it a good, thorough review, shall we? Let's find out how you did in the courage factor.

What opportunities have you missed because you were afraid?

What are the top 3 things you didn't do because fear got in your way?

Are you feeling regretful about any of the events that transpired in your life this last year?

What would you do differently if given a chance?

How has your inability to take action stopped you from getting what you want out of life?

What is your biggest fear right in this moment?

How is this affecting your current situation and how it will affect your future?

By examining the things that held you back in the past, you'll be able to gain perspective on how you can change and shape your future. Really use these questions and answers to help you decide how you want to move forward from this moment. Then go for all the glory!

"A Lil More Exercise On Courage"

List three things you can do this week to practice being courageous. This week, at the top of my list, is to submit a proposal to ghostwrite a book for a high profile figure. I've been working on the proposal for weeks, but I've never ghostwritten before. Am I good enough? I think I am. *Will he?* I don't know – but if I don't submit the proposal I'll never know! Your turn, what's on your list?

1. _____.

2. _____.

3. _____.

Okay, friend, you've got your list together, so now you *have* to go out and do it! But before you go, let me ask you to do one final exercise. Picture yourself at your 95th birthday party. All your family and friends have gathered to celebrate your life. What will everyone have to say about you? When they put on the "This Is Your Life" skit, who's showing up and what did you do? Now go and fulfill that vision.

Let's Wrap It Up

- ✔ Courage as defined by me, is the ability to face a difficult moment despite fear.

- ✔ To gain perspective and learn how you can change snd shape your future, first examine your last 12 months and determine what held you back.

- ✔ You don't have to conquer your fear, you just have to push past it.

- ✔ When in doubt, apply the 3 steps of courage by default:
    1. Delegate whatever you can.
    2. Practice distraction techniques.
    3. Use the fear as fuel to propel past the challenge

- ✔ Once you start moving past the fear, your success factor soars exponentially.

- ✔ Get your finances in check, make a plan, take the risk.

Notes:

_____
_____
_____
_____
_____
_____

Resilience

*"Man never made any material as resilient
as the human spirit."*
– Bernard Williams

The Human Spirit

The human spirit is that little voice you hear that tells you, *"Don't give up." "Just hold on." "Give it one more go."* It's the part of you that pushes you when you feel all hope is lost. It's how you keep moving forward when everything in the world keeps trying to push you back. The more risks you take, the more your spirit is challenged. When you are successful, your spirit grows stronger. Though you may not realize it in the moment, your spirit also grows when you fail. You become more resilient with each experience, be it failure or success. To help put things into perspective, make a list of your successes and your failures. Don't be stingy with your success list either. If you graduated kindergarten, that goes in the list of success. If you got your G.E.D., congratulations, you succeeded! I realize that sounds pedestrian, perhaps even a bit silly, but believe me, it works. Jot down every single achievement. How does your list look? Of course you also need to examine your shortcomings because they too have provided you with valuable knowledge and experience. What has been your greatest failure to date? How did those experiences shape your life? How have they made you more resilient? How has your spirit been affected by your achievements and shortcomings?

"Get Over It"

Resilience is defined as, "the ability to recover after deformation caused especially by compressive stress."[3] Resilience is a key component to achieving your goals, dreams, desires and ultimate success. You need to be able to bounce back after life puts your butt in a hot box and starts pressing on every side. Now, don't you just hate when the compression is hitting you at every side and people come up and tell you, *"Get over it?"* If it were that easy, you'd already be over whatever it is you're still under. Right? Your lover leaves you and all your friends tell you, "Oh, just get over it." You lose a job or get passed over for a promotion, and people who have no idea what you have invested in the situation are in your ear telling you, *"Just get over it."* It's enough to drive a person mad. But sometimes it's exactly what we need to hear. Keep reading to find out why.

"You Can Handle More Than You Think"

Humans are emotional beings and our spirits can be quite irrational. We want to *feel.* We thrive on emotion, and yes, even drama. Then, once we have drama in our lives, we start crying and complaining, kicking and screaming, *"I just can't take it anymore."* But, we don't give ourselves enough credit as to just how much we can endure. I'm about to get a little spiritual on you, so just hold on. An old proverb I've been told all my life is, *"God doesn't give you more than you can handle."* Are you thinking, *"Hmm, I don't know about that?"* Well, spirituality aside, it doesn't matter who you believe in, because that proverb is true. You will never, in this lifetime, be given more than you can handle. Yes, there will be times when it *feels* like too much to bear, but when it's all said and done, if you allow your spirit to push through, you *will* get over it and you'll be stronger for it in the long run. When your people tell you

---

3   www.merriam-webster.com/dictionary/resilience

"*Get over it,*" curse them under your breath if you must, but take their advice. You will survive; you will overcome, so get over it already!

"How Do I Just Get Over It?"

How do you get over disappointment, failure, loss, frustration, heartbreak, and all of life's other trials and tribulations? It's hard to say. Because we are all individual, spiritual, emotional beings, we each react and respond differently to the stresses of life. Duh. That rationale is no help. I know. The truth is, it's virtually impossible to just throw your hands up in the air and "get over it." Like most things, it's a process and it takes time. But there are a few ways you can help speed things along and save yourself from going into the deep, dark hole of disappointment.

1. Find your outlet.

Distraction can be an extremely powerful tool when you are trying to get over something. When you allow your thoughts, time and attention to be occupied by other things, you aren't left with much time to focus on the problem. It's sort of like when you have a headache and then stub your toe. You suddenly forget the pain in your head and focus on your toe. Likewise, joining a cooking class, a running group, signing up for yoga, sweeping the floors, or whatever else tickles your fancy can be very helpful when you're trying to get over something. Just be sure to get involved in an activity that is engaging. Whenever I'm upset or trying to get over something, I wash dishes. P.S. Let me just say that on an ordinary day, I hate washing dishes, but when I want to get over something, I find it to be a very cathartic activity. Interestingly, this is usually when I have my best ideas. There is a small caveat: if the activity or distraction you choose leaves your mind open to obsess about the situation, then that tells you your activity isn't fun or engaging enough. Go find your fun and give it a whirl!

2. Call in for backup.

Assemble your posse and tell them it's time to show you some love. Don't be scared to tell your friends exactly what kind of support you need. There's no shame in telling someone, *"Friend, I need some support, but here's what I don't need..."* Maybe you need them to help throw you a pity party, talk the night away with you as you drown your sorrows in a gallon of ice cream or beer or take you out for a long run. If they are truly your friends, they'll be there in any fashion you need. In Chapter 6, we'll talk more about friends and how having the right circle is key to your success. Stay tuned.

3. Get into action.

There's nothing like a little (or big) disappointment to get you fired up and amped to prove your offenders wrong. Harness all your feelings of anger, sorrow, disappointment or whatever other emotions you're experiencing and roll it all into one power-packed ball of action. If you didn't get the promotion, now is your chance to get back to work and do your job with more passion and vigor than ever; show them how good you really are and what a mistake they made. Or better yet, bump up your resume and go after a better job. Getting into action is all about self-improvement. Whatever you're trying to get over will seem really insignificant once you focus on yourself and the ways you can improve your overall life experience. Get out there and take action – whether in love, career, relationships or yourself – there is room for improvement and this is the opportunity for you to work on it.

While none of these steps are answers to the problem, they will help you get over it and allow you to recognize there is a much bigger picture, one truly worth investing your time and energy. Make the decision that no matter what comes your way. You and your spirit are going to absorb compression and bounce back into your original form. You may even emerge as a more upgraded version of yourself.

"The 24-Hour Rule"

There's a little something I teach my coaching clients called the 24-hour rule. Basically, the rule states that you are allowed to feel angry, sad, mad, depressed, sorry for yourself, or whatever other emotion you need to feel regarding a particular situation for 24 hours

Nothing lasts forever, so whatever issue you're having, remember, it's *temporary*.

and only 24 hours. Believe it or not, it's healthy to be sad. It's healthy to have a good cry, to scream your head off or even break a few plates if need be. It's therapeutic. I gotta admit, as a fiery Puerto Rican, I've broken a few dishes in my day and boy was it liberating! I don't recommend you start breaking the fine china, but you get my drift. Don't be afraid to express yourself and really feel the feelings you have over a disappointment, loss or setback. Mourning the situation is good for the soul. *"Nothing lasts forever, so whatever issue you're having, remember, it's temporary."* So you go ahead and take your 24 hours. After that, you have to put your big girl panties or your big boy underoos back on and get back to work.

The Path to Resilience – My Personal Story

"*I am a failure!*" I cried to my husband. "*I am failing every single day. I'm home all day and I can't get this house cleaned, I can't finish my book, I don't do enough activities with the baby, my business isn't growing fast enough and I'm costing our family money. I can't do this anymore!*" I poured my heart and soul out to my husband that evening. I was in pain. Deep, gut-wrenching pain. I hurt so much that my soul hurt. I believed every single word of my plea in that moment. I was burning with internal conflict and there was no resolution in sight. I had considered quitting my business and getting a "real" job, but I couldn't bring myself to apply anywhere. I knew that if I got hired I'd never take my business where I wanted it to go. I was resistant to quitting but desperate to find a way out of my situation. How was I going to succeed? Would I ever get to the point where I'd be an asset to our family?

Believe it or not, those were the foolish thoughts that ran through my head that evening. My husband, bless his heart, was extremely supportive. He told me he'd support me no matter what I decided. If I quit the business, he'd be cool and if I stuck it out he'd be equally happy. But would I? Immediately, I realized the answer was no. No, I definitely would not be happy if I gave up on myself and my dreams. In that moment, I was enlightened with the knowledge that balance does not exist when you're going for the glory. I had to give myself permission to leave a few dishes behind, to let the laundry build up for a week or two, and to fail a little bit. Heck, I had to give myself permission to fail a lot. It was all part of the journey. It was all for the greater cause. I decided right then and there – dishes be damned! I could handle the pressures, I would make the best decision for myself and my family in that moment and I wouldn't beat myself up if I fell short in any area.

I allowed my spirit to push me through that very dark, difficult evening and I've never looked back. Today, my business has its ups and downs just like any other, but my family and I have never been happier. We weathered the storms and we'll continue to do so, knowing that being able to bounce back from trials and tribulations is what keeps up strong.

"I haven't failed. I've just found 10,000 ways that won't work." - Thomas Edison

Failure is a necessary part of success. It's kind of like dating. If you don't date a loser or two in your lifetime, you never learn to appreciate a good man or woman. It's also a great learning tool. Each time an approach or method on your pursuit to success fails, you've just gained knowledge and experience. It's easy to feel defeated or depressed as a result of failure but it's important to mitigate the situation immediately and look for the blessing. What have you learned? What could you have done differently? How will this failure help you in the future? These questions might be hard to answer at first glance, but it's important to keep circling back to them until you have the answers. If you're having trouble answering these questions then I'll tell you bluntly, you're not going deep enough. You have all the answers within yourself and, "I don't know" is not a valid answer. It's a cop out – and I'm calling you out on it.

Take a hint from the U.S. Marine Corps. They use a tool called an after-action report which is completed after every exercise or conflict. This report helps commanders learn what did and didn't work. It doesn't matter if the mission was a success or a failure; a report is conducted at the conclusion to improve efforts for the future. They even have a center devoted to learning from missions called the Center for Lessons Learned. If it's good enough for the U.S. Marine Corps, America's 911 Force, then certainly it could help you out as well. Develop your own after-action report and start your own "center for lessons learned" file.

My Personal After-Action Report

My greatest failure to date was...

I failed because...

The things I did right were...

The things I could have done better were...

This failure has helped my success because now...

Next time I'll...

And there you have it. Your personal after action report that you can change or modify according to your needs. Once you've figured out what doesn't work, you can get back to the drawing board and devise a new plan, one that will work and help you develop an attitude of resilience. Do that and you'll rise to success that much faster.

I know I'm making you do a lot of work in this book with all these questions and fill in the blank activities, but I promise you, do the work and you'll see your dreams really are within your reach.

"Stop The Insanity"

We've talked about the benefits of learning from failure and developing a winning plan based on lessons learned. What's not part of the plan? Doing the same thing over and over again, expecting different results. According to Albert Einstein, that's the definition of insanity! Have you ever displayed acts of insanity? You know you have. I am raising my hand high in the sky because, believe me, I have been insane one too many times in this life. Have you dated the same type of person over and over again, only to wonder why you still haven't found – the "one"? Have you floated from one dead-end job to another? Have you tried to build your business or gain clients using the same methodologies over and over without much success? Well, to quote 90's sensation and fitness guru Susan Powter, "Stop the insanity!" Whatever you've been doing clearly isn't working. Why have you been allowing yourself to fall into the same trap? Don't you love yourself enough to break the cycle? Don't you know your worth and value? Is your self-esteem and confidence so low that you're willing to allow yourself to be short-changed in life? If you've been in a holding pattern with a life that feels less than wonderful, **"When the game changes, you've** you can go ahead **got to change your game."** and safely answer no, no, and yes. Clearly you don't love yourself, you don't know you're worth and your self-esteem and confidence are so low that you're blinded to your potential. I know there's a reader or two out there who has become so accustomed to this lifestyle that he or she is probably thinking, *"I do love myself and I'm confident but..."* followed by a myriad of excuses such as, *"I have responsibilities and right now I can't afford to make a change." "I don't have the time right now." "I don't have the resources." "I'm too old to start over."* Blah, blah, blah. That's what I say to those excuses! You are stronger and better than that, my friend. If you want change bad enough, you'll find a way to overcome each and every one of those excuses. More importantly, if you love yourself, then you have no choice but to abolish those excuses. It's time to mix it up. Change the game plan. As one of my mentors, Marie Forleo says,"*When the game changes, you've got to change your game.*"

This where developing resilience really comes into play. If every time you suffer a setback or stop taking forward action to sulk in the corner for a day, a week, a month or a year, you are being counter-productive and ultimately, sabotaging yourself. This is not the time to have a pity-party or wallow in your sorrows and excuses. Rejection and failure are not valid reasons to throw in the towel or to cower away. They are the incentive, the kindling you need to fuel the fire **A little failure equals a lot of success.** and turn up the heat on your resilience and passion.

Remember, you *can* and *will* bounce back from any challenge or obstacle if you remain open to the notion that failure is important to success. Get off your butt, take some action and fail a little bit. "*A little failure equals a lot of success.*"

"Asking The Hard Questions"

If you haven't figured it out yet, a great deal of this book is all about soul searching and asking yourself some deep, dark questions to deal with some things you probably really don't want to deal with. This is the perfect time for you to practice getting over it and pushing forward. Ask yourself the following questions:

How resilient am I?

How do I handle stress?

What do I do when things get tough?

What excuses have I been making over and over?

How do I "power through" and keep moving forward?

Once you've written down your answers, take a few minutes to reflect and see where your weak spots are on the resilience factor. Some of us have been built to handle an extreme amount of stress and some of us can only tolerate about a teaspoonful at a time. No matter what category you fall into, learning to be a resilient individual is vital. When it comes to life success, it's not the strong that survive; it's the resilient.

"It's All About Peace"

Think about a recent setback, heartbreak or failure. How long did it take you to bounce back? What helped you get over it? If you're not over it, what about the situation is making it impossible to let go? How can you rectify it? What has to happen for you to find peace? **The key to resilience comes from finding peace in the situation.** "The key to resilience comes from finding peace in the situation." Perhaps you need closure with an ex, maybe you need to hear your boss's rationale for passing you up for promotion or maybe you need a friend to give you reassurance. Find peace and your resilience will blossom.

Sometimes, we're not in a position where we can get the closure we're hoping to find. You might desperately want to close the door on an old flame, but have no way of reaching him. Maybe you haven't gotten over an emotional wound from years past and you have no way of finding a third party to help you find the answers you need. Without sugar-coating it, I'll be straight up – these situations suck. The only thing left to do is find the answers within. Every thing you experience in life comes with a purpose. Sometimes, it's to help you learn to deal with a challenge. It might have been something you needed to experience in order for you to be a testimony for someone else. Whatever the case may be, remember, you *do* have the answers. If you get honest with yourself, you'll know what you need to do to find peace. Here's a bone for you to chew on: if you're still having trouble finding peace, maybe you need to check your ego. Our ego has a way of playing amazing tricks on us and can make us feel that we cared more about a person, place or thing more than we actually did. In reality, our ego is just upset that we lost. How is your ego affecting your ability to find peace? The ego is a dream killer, so beware and put that bad boy in check.

Let's Wrap It Up

- ✔ You've been more successful than perhaps you give yourself credit.

- ✔ When your friends tell you to "get over it," take their advice and follow the 3 steps:
    1. Find your outlet.
    2. Call in for back up.
    3. Get into action.

- ✔ If something isn't working, change your game plan and find what works.

- ✔ Rejection and failure are not valid reasons to throw in the towel.

- ✔ Find peace in your situation and your resilience will blossom.

- ✔ Check your ego.

Notes:

_____
_____
_____
_____
_____
_____

༺❀༻

Authenticity

"Often people attempt to live their lives backwards; they try to have more things, or more money in order to do more of what they want, so they will be happier. The way it actually works is the reverse. You must first be who you really are, then do what you need to do, in order to have what you want."

- Margaret Young

"Inherited Dreams"

Most parents want more for their children. All of us want our children to grow up having more than we had and to become more than we became. We hope that the dreams we have for our children will come to fruition so we impress upon them our desires. We talk to them about the importance of following a particular path that will help them achieve the dreams we have for them. In essence, our children inherit our dreams. Perhaps you can think of a dream your parents had that was passed onto you. What marks of success were passed down to you as a child? My mom believed success meant graduating college and getting a job in corporate America that provided benefits and "security." My father's motto was, "Education first, boys second." According to my parents, as long as I graduated college I would be successful. I laugh thinking about it. Graduating college is a great stepping-stone for success, but it's not the only path to get there. **Sidenote:** If you have the opportunity to go to college, you should consider giving it a go. Aside from opening many doors, it's also a good experience in general. Please don't think I'm telling you not to go to college. I'm just saying if you didn't go or if you can't go, that doesn't mean you won't be successful. It just means you might have to work a little harder and/or find opportunities through other avenues. Just look at Bill Gates, Mark Zuckerburg and many other wildly successful individuals. They didn't graduate college, but they did achieve amazing things. All things are possible; some things just take a few extra steps.

Inherited dreams can be good because they can function as guiding lights, but knowing the difference between *your* dream and the dreams that have been passed onto you is critical. If you have to choose between one dream or someone else's, make sure you follow your own dreams. Pursuing someone else's dream will leave you frustrated, angry and unfulfilled. It will waste your time and drain your energy. In the end, you will always have a void that will never be filled because you aren't following your heart. You may want to ask yourself these reflective questions to determine if your present life is in alignment with YOUR dream life:

Are you in a job you *love*?

Do you really *want* to work in your 9 – 5 job, or are you staying because it's what your partner wants?

Is there something you'd rather be studying in school?

Are you living someone else's dream?

A major component of authenticity is following your personal ambitions – not those impressed upon you by others. To quote the late, great Steve Jobs, "Your time is limited, so don't waste it living someone else's life." Maybe you already knew that, but if you're reading this book, there's a good chance you need to hear it again.

"Your Authentic Self"

Celebrity psychiatrist Dr. Phil, defines authentic self as, "being who you were created to be." That's a pretty deep concept. Most of us have no clue what we want to eat for dinner let alone know who we were created to be. Honestly, when I first heard the term "authentic self" I rolled my eyes and thought, 'Here we go. More kumbaya, I love Mother Nature, twilight zone-music-in-the-background, crap!' In fact, I resisted this term for several years because quite frankly, it felt too intimate. I didn't want to ask myself the tough questions associated with discovering my authentic self. It was uncomfortable. Who was I really? Had I become the person I thought I'd be? Was I being the real me? Was I following my dreams? Are you?

"When we were living in Stafford, VA for a short time I had a really difficult time finding work. I knew that we really needed me to have a job in order to make ends meet so I just started applying for anything in the help wanted ads. I ended up getting hired to clean a family's home.

This woman was a stay-at-home mom, but she did the books for her husband's business, was in charge of countless clubs at school for her over-achieving daughter and had a farm to run because her husband was gone so much. I found that I was extremely embarrassed to tell anyone what I was doing for work and that I was becoming depressed.

This was the furthest I had ever strayed from following my heart in something I was doing. I remember lying in bed crying myself to sleep one night when my husband awoke and asked me what was wrong...all I could tell him was, 'This job is hurting my soul.' I could tell he thought it was a slight exaggeration, but I'm telling you now - that job was slowly killing who I knew I was meant NOT to be!

I promised myself after that to be more focused, finished my degree, and never be back in that situation again."

- Sarah Haught Pevehouse of ThereSheGoes.org

For me, hindsight has been 20/20. When I think back on who I was during my high school and college years I shudder to think of the person I was desperately trying to be. I got sidetracked and let the need to "fit in" take over. In retrospect, a lot of my true friends really didn't like me during that period of my life. How ironic. I was destroying myself to impress them and all along, they just wanted the "regular" me. I learned the very hard way that it's more important to impress myself rather than those around me.

You'll see that when you show your authentic self, the people who add the most value to your life will stay by your side. They will uplift you, encourage you and help you shine brighter than those other people who do not appreciate the value of the real you. Not being true to yourself, who you are at your core, means you are missing out on the greatest life you could possibly have. I missed out on many of my dreams because I was too busy pursuing inherited dreams and trying to follow the pack. What are you missing out on, or what have you missed out on because you didn't honor your authentic self?

"What You Do Is Not Who You Are"

Apart from following others or trying to portray ourselves as someone we're not, the other trap we fall prey to is allowing our profession to take over our identity. Have you ever gone to a job interview and been asked the question, *"Tell me about yourself?"* What is the correct response? Do you share your love of dancing in the rain? No, of course not. You give the winning speech you've meticulously prepared that showcases your relevant work experience and strengths that directly relate to the position. In short, you give them the highlights of your resume. While this is appropriate in an interview, going around allowing your identity to be your curriculum vitae is not. *"Newsflash: what you do professionally is not who you are."* If you find yourself giving people a synopsis of your professional life rather than sharing who you really are, it might be

Newsflash: what you do professionally is not who you are.

time to take a step back and ask yourself, *"Have I gotten so caught up making a living that I've forgotten to have a life?"* Are you honoring your authentic self? Do you share who you are at your core with others? Are you filling your spare time with activities that uplift and fill you with passion or are you spending every waking moment focused on your career? Being ambitious is a great character trait, but being too ambitious can also hinder your authenticity and may ultimately affect your relationships with the people you care about most. It can take over and force you to sacrifice things that are truly important to you. How can you be more authentic in your day-to-day life? Is there a way to find, dare I say it, "balance?"

"An Authentically Balanced Life"

No. In my opinion there is no such thing as a balanced life. There will always be one thing or another that needs a little more of your time and attention than you have or would like to give. But – when you choose to honor your authentic self and devote the time and attention to the things that will bring you joy or satisfaction, you will feel a sense of balance. Personally, I always feel guilty about not doing a load of laundry every day. My life would be perfectly balanced if I could just manage to get everything done that needs to get done, give my babies lots of undivided attention and wash, fold and put away one load of laundry every single day. Never happens. And yet, I feel blissfully balanced. Things get done as they need to get done, and meanwhile, I do what feels right for me in the moment. I'm sure washing that load of laundry will feel right when I'm down to my last bra and panty set.

So, my dear friend, don't get too caught up on having a "balanced life." Focus on doing what works for you while you honor your authentic self, dreams and goals.

"Don't Imitate, Originate"

What is imitation? Imitation is the antithesis of authenticity. It's a copy. Rarely has a copy ever been better than the original. Am I telling the truth or what? You know I am. When was the last time you bought a bootleg video that looked better than a blue ray? Okay, so you've never bought a bootleg (wink, wink) because that would be illegal. But I'm just saying, we can agree that the quality of a copy is never quite as good as the original. Even though we know this to be true, a part of us can't resist the desire to imitate others. From fashion to food, home décor to diet fads, most of us can't help but follow the pack. If Vogue Magazine were to suggest wearing a fur coat in 98-degree heat, you can bet your hard-earned dollar there would be one or two fools out there rocking that coat. Why? Because Vogue said so. This is the kind of person who ends up going down with heat stroke in the name of fashion. It sounds ridiculous, doesn't it? That's because it is! Imitating others is foolish; it robs you of your authenticity and might even make you look a bit silly. Which brings me to another very important message

Look straight-ahead and go after what *you* want, not what you think you should want because of what others have.

I need you to wrap your head around: Stop trying to keep up with the Joneses! Don't look to your left, don't look to your right. Forget about what your neighbor is doing or what they have. "*Look straight-ahead and go after what you want, not what you think you should want because of what others have.*"

Recently, I witnessed how this mentality of 'keeping up' was affecting a friend's business. My sweet friend, let's call her Marissa,* had been building her business for several months with steady progression. She had achieved good growth and was on par with the goals she had set for herself when she first started out. Then along came a new kid on the block. The new kid took the business by storm and raised the bar in a major way. To Marissa, it felt as though her competitor's business model might destroy her business. Every

---

Names have been changed.

day she would obsess on the idea that her competition was going to "shut her down" and that her dreams of having a successful business were slowly slipping away. As the outsider looking in I could see that the competition, despite doing a great job of taking the market by storm, really wasn't going to put my friend out of business. Marissa was going to put *herself* out of business because she couldn't focus on anything other than what her competitor was doing. She was forgetting to take care of the most important element of her company's success, her client! She was stressing herself beyond belief, which in turn was affecting her home life. Her thoughts were centered around the things her competition was achieving rather than thinking on how she could set herself apart. After several conversations, Marissa finally got it. She came around and realized she had two choices – she could either focus on the competition and watch as her business crashed and burned, or she could focus on ways she and her team could better serve the market. Thankfully, she chose the latter. She recently achieved a milestone in her business and has positioned herself to be a leader in her industry. The lesson I want you to take away is this: "*Stop obsessing over what others have and instead give gratitude for what you have*."

Stop obsessing over what others have and instead give gratitude for what you have.

You have a life, talent, ambition and the ability to achieve anything you set your mind to. Break away from the norm, don't focus on the competition, and brainstorm ways you can set yourself apart from everyone else by being exactly who you are.

I feel an exercise coming on. Do you feel it too? Yup, here it is. Make a list of the things you feel make you, *you*. Are you funny, witty, sarcastic? Do you have an exceptional work ethic? Are you a laissez-faire type of person, a sort of go-with-the-flow type? There are all types of characteristics that make people who they are. Don't be afraid to list even the quirky things – maybe you wear bright purple socks all the time. Look at world-renowned chef, Mario Batale and his orange clogs. They've become a trademark, an essential part of his brand. What about Carrot Top? Remember him? Back in the early 90's the comedian Carrot Top was able to make a name for himself by capitalizing on his bright red, curly hair and ridiculously built body. Your list should include all kinds of traits both physical and character. If you have trouble coming up with your traits, then phone a friend. Ask your buddies to give you a word or two that describe you. Your list will begin to take shape soon enough. Don't skip this exercise because it's going to help you In the next section. Now get started on your list. I am...

_____

_____

_____

_____

_____

_____

What did you learn about yourself? How can these traits set you apart from others? If this task was difficult for you, that's okay. It can be a challenge to take a look at ourselves and find our unique qualities. Don't worry. Just keep at it, heck, feel free to come back and add to it as you think of things.

"Your Authentic Brand"

Whether you're building a business or looking for a career change, you've got to create and develop your brand. In chapter 10 you're going to get the meat and potatoes of building your brand, but I want you to start thinking about the authentic elements that make up who you are. Take a look at the last section and review the list of traits that make you, you. I told you you'd need the exercise to help you with this section, so if you didn't do it, go back and do it now. This list of traits will be a dynamic list, meaning that as you evolve and grow, it may change. Roll with it and accept the change. Try and honor this list in all that you do, because the more authentic you stay, the more authentic your brand will be. The more authentic a brand you have, the more success you will attract. We're going to keep building on this, so hang tight.

"The Common Denominator"

As I was researching for this book I had the opportunity to interview many successful people, I watched hours upon hours of video footage (read: many, many episodes of E-True Hollywood stories) to cherry-pick the best examples of successful people and decode just exactly what they did to come out ahead of the pack. Hands down, the common denominator for every successful person was that they all stayed true to themselves. They knew exactly what they wanted, they knew who they were, and they weren't willing to compromise or settle until they got what they were after. Being themselves is exactly what propelled them to the top.

That's your takeaway from this chapter. You being you is what makes your life richer than any dollar bill ever will. When you are true to yourself and do the things you really love, the money follows. Jealousy, envy and daydreaming about other people's success, achievements and materials do nothing but make you look ugly. It's not a pretty picture and *no*, you don't look cute. Let me drive **Be who you are. Do what you love. The money will follow.** the moral of this chapter home to you one more time, just in case you missed it: *"Be who you are. Do what you love. The money will follow."* Got it? Good!

"Diggin' Down And Dirty"

It's your favorite part of the chapters, the getting down and dirty in a steamy Q&A session with your soul. Fill in the answers as openly and honestly as possible.

When are you most yourself?

When have you hidden the "real" you from others? How did that affect you?

If you've ever been guilty of trying to 'keep up with the Jones'' (and you know you have!), how can you eliminate that line of thinking from now on?

What is the one thing or trait you have that you wish others could see and appreciate?

Going forward, how will you show this off and allow others to see you shine?

Let's Wrap It Up

- ✔ Inherited dreams stop us from reaching our full potential. Identify your inherited dreams, then choose to follow your own.

- ✔ Being your "authentic self" means being who you were created to be.

- ✔ What you do professionally does not define who you are.

- ✔ Don't imitate others. Be your original self.

- ✔ Stop obsessing over what others have and give gratitude for what you have.

- ✔ The more authentic your brand is, the more success you will have.

- ✔ Be who you are. Love what you do. The money will follow.

Notes:

_____

_____

_____

_____

_____

_____

Perseverance

"Accept that all of us can be hurt, that all of us can- and surely will at times-fail. Other vulnerabilities, like being embarrassed or risking love, can be terrifying too. I think we should follow a simple rule: if we can take the worst, take the risk."
— Dr. Joyce Brothers

"If We Can Take The Worst, Take The Risk."

How much can any of us take? When is enough struggle, enough pain, enough failure, *enough*? Only you know how much you can take. No one can make that determination for you, yet so often, we give people in our lives the power to make these decisions. We allow people to tell us, *"You've given it a good run. It's okay to quit now."* Or we nod in agreement when a confidante tells us, *"You shouldn't keep subjecting yourself to failure. Maybe it's time to move on and find something else."* In that moment, when you're feeling down and out, even if you know you've still got a bit of fight left in you, hearing your support system telling you to give up makes it difficult to resist the urge to quit. It can almost seem too much to bear when every door seems to be shutting in your face and you take into consideration all you've invested and sacrificed to pursue this dream. But it doesn't have to be. You *can* take the worst. You can take whatever comes your way. You have the potential to shut out the rest of the world and go for yours. Take the good, take the bad, take the worst, take the risk. In the words of Bethenny Frankel, *"Hardship is better than regret."*

"Do The Work — Make Your Break"

There's no way around it. If you want to succeed you have to be willing to do the work and do everything you can to make your breaks. Let me expand on these principles. When I say you must be willing to do the work, I mean it. These days, people seem to be looking to do the least amount possible, yet want all the rewards. It makes no sense. I'm all for working smarter not harder, but you still have to *do the work!* Those who regularly demonstrate they can and are willing to get down to business always stand out above the rest. You're going to have some hard times – so what? Isn't working your butt off for a little while worth the reward of having all your dreams come true?

Now, I'm going to warn you: a little bit of a contradiction is coming up. Bear with me as we navigate through the double standard. Being the first person in and the last person out of the office counts for a lot, but personally, I don't really care for that school of thought. Why not? Because I don't think you should *have* to be in an office 18 hours a day or work on building your business 20 hours a day to prove you're good. I know from experience that if you show up for your eight hour work shift and work your tail off, efficiently and effectively, you are *way* better than the schmuck next to you who is in the office until 8pm but hasn't accomplished half the amount of work you have. Are you tracking with me? Sadly, every now and again the environment you're in demands you put "face time" in at the office. Or perhaps you're about to launch a new product for your business and you actually need every minute of

But if you must work to the bone, do it with passion. Do it with joy.

a 20-hour day. Sometimes you have to go to a networking event on an evening when all you want to do is crash out. These are the moments when perseverance matters. It's a conundrum. What to do? Do you bust your butt during an 8-hr day and call it quits at 5pm or do you rack up 100-hour workweeks? Honestly, do what you have to do – whatever is right for your particular situation, goal or ambition. For your sanity, I encourage you to try and capitalize your time and set yourself apart as a highly efficient and effective individual. *"But if you must work to the bone, do it with passion. Do it with joy."* That's part of being perseverant; giving your best even when you don't feel you're getting the reward or recognition you deserve. If you continue to persevere – to work to your maximum potential – you *will* achieve success. That brings us to making your break.

Everyone hopes for a "big break," the perfect job, a meeting with a top agent, the "gig of a lifetime" or what have you. We've become so used to Hollywood romanticizing the notion of being "discovered" that we've actually started to believe the answer to all our prayers comes in the form of a "big break." Ha! If you're waiting for your big break to come along, you are in for a long wait my friend. Sure, it's possible. *Anything* is possible, but is it likely? Probably not. If you want to get discovered, you need to get motivated and put yourself in a position to be discovered. If you want to land the perfect job, you have to create an opportunity that will allow you to connect with someone in that company and then give the interview of your life. You can even win the lotto and hit the mega millions, but it'll never happen unless you buy a ticket and *play* the lotto.

The tough part about making your own breaks is that it comes with a lot of potential for disappointment and rejection. You really need to put yourself out there. You're out of your comfort zone and you're taking a risk hoping the person in the position to help you will **When a door closes in your face, go around the back and climb in through a window.** respond. Again, this is where a spirit of perseverance really pays off. When the inevitable happens, and you experience a setback, a rejection or perhaps even a failure, you must persevere. *"When a door closes in your face, go* *around the back and climb in through a window."* Just as Michael Bloomberg, 108th Mayor of New York City and founder of Bloomberg LP once said, *"I have never feared failure or hard work."* Don't be afraid. Go for it. Put yourself out there because no matter what the outcome, at least then you'll know.

---

3 Ways to Make Your Break:

1. Share your passion.
Start spreading the word to everyone you meet about your intentions and plans. You never know whom you'll meet or whom you're speaking with.

2. Be prepared.
Have your portfolio, business card, monologue, etc. prepared and ready to roll. Opportunities are knocking at every corner. Be ready to shine.

3. Search for opportunities.
Your break is waiting for you. All you have to do is look for it. Join a group, conduct a Google search, volunteer – you get the drift. There are plenty of opportunities to be had. Go get them!

"Success: Easy To Achieve, Hard To Maintain"

Did you think the "hard" part was achieving success? I thought so too. Boy, were we wrong. Attaining success once is the simple task. Think about "one-hit wonders." These artists grace our airwaves with a super catchy beat, make us fall in love with a song and then fade into obscurity, never to be heard from again. Why does this happen? I'll tell you why. Coming up with a catchy beat and a good hook is the easy part. Add to the mix a great marketing strategy and you're golden. But once that train pulls out of the station, it's gone. Finding the next big thing is where the challenge lies. Making us fall in love with them over and over again is the struggle. That's probably why 1 in 2 marriages fail. Because it's hard work to keep making our partners fall in love with us over and over again – but hey, that's for another book.

Let's consider runners. To be able to run one mile in 5 minutes is amazing. Now imagine keeping that same 5-minute per mile pace for an entire 26.2 miles marathon. At that pace, the runner would finish the marathon in 2 hours and 11 minutes. That's bananas! But hold onto your pants, because get this: the world record for running a marathon is currently 2 hours, 3 minutes and 2 seconds.[4] There is someone in this world that *maintains* a successful pace of less than 5-minutes per mile for over 26 miles. How do runners do it? I'll tell ya, it's not exactly rocket science. Marathon runners, especially the elite runners, are able to maintain their successful pace because they 1) work hard, 2) stay consistent and 3) remain perseverant even when their bodies feel like they might possibly collapse. Yes, there are those who are naturally gifted, but even the most talented train and condition themselves. Elite runners know that being successful in a race is about maintaining a consistent pace.

"Consistency Is Key"

Typically, I work with women, but every now and again a man will grace my virtual office with his presence. Along came a new prospective client – let's call him James*. James wanted help getting organized and staying on track. He was also hoping that our work together would result in him getting a promotion. When we met, James had already been employed for several years and should have been promoted two years prior. His lack of consistency had led to his not getting promoted in a timely manner. As we

---

4   www.baa.org/races/boston-marathon.aspx

chatted about his habits, several things became very clear. 1. James was always late. 2. He was very good about starting a project, but never following through. 3. He was excellent at giving lip service. I summed all of this up by pointing out to James that he was consistently inconsistent. He talked the talk, but rarely walked the walk. He laughed at the idea, but agreed – he knew his issue was consistency, or lack thereof. In the end, James and I agreed we were not a match made in coaching heaven. You see, James was not ready to get consistent. He really didn't want to change his ways, nor did he want to be committed to a program that would force him to be on time or stretch him out of his comfort zone. I still keep in touch with James from time to time, and though he hasn't gotten that promotion yet, I'm sure he'll get there one day. He has extraordinary potential and is a very hard worker when he applies himself. Had he been able to demonstrate his work ethic and go-getter spirit consistently, I am very certain James would have been promoted ages ago.

I shared this story with you to stress the importance of consistency. The most successful businesses are built by people who are consistent. They have a systematic approach to making things happen. They follow through on tasks and most importantly; they do something each and every day to help them get one step closer to their goal. Successful people do what they have to do even when they don't feel like it. How consistent are you in pursuing your goals? How persistent are you when it comes to going after what you want? What triggers you to be inconsistent? Identify where your sabotage lies and work on developing systems to combat it. If you're trying to lose weight and you have a killer sweet tooth, make sure you're not bringing sweets into the house and get your friends on board to keep you away from the cookie jar. If you are like James and are constantly late, be sure to set multiple alarm clocks and write everything

Do something every single day to help you reach your dream, even when you don't feel like it.

in your planner 15 minutes before the actual start time. You get the idea. Make the decision right now to step up your consistency game. *"Do something every single day to help you reach your dream, even when you don't feel like it."*

"Don't Be A P.I.T.A"

Perseverance is key, but it doesn't mean being a P.I.T.A aka Pain In The Ass. If you are trying to get featured in a magazine or looking to get hired by a company, you should definitely reach out and touch base, but don't bombard the key point of contact and become a royal P.I.T.A. That's a fast-track way to being put on the black list. No, perseverance is all about working hard, making the right connections, approaching people with the right tact and moving forward despite rejection.

"There Are No Guarantees In Life"

While there are no guarantees in life, I will guarantee you this one thing: whether or not you achieve your vision of success as planned, you will without a doubt feel an unparalleled level of success knowing that you gave it your all *if* you do the things we discuss in this book. Perseverance is about going the distance, despite the odds. It's about staying focused on your destination while embarking on the journey of a lifetime. The satisfaction you will gain from knowing you never quit, even when the going got really tough, will in itself be success.

"Don't Be fooled, It Will Get Really, Freakin' Tough!"

It's going to happen. One day, heck, maybe even one month is going to be really, really, freakin' crappy. Nothing is going to go your way, every door is going to slam in your face, all the windows of opportunity are going to have those metal bars like the windows in the ghetto and you're going to want to quit. Don't! That's going to be the moment you're going to have to dig down deep and remind yourself why you started the journey in the first place. When we write things down, we tend to remember them better. So write it down now.

Why are you pursuing this goal?

What will it mean to you when you finally fulfill your dream?

How will you feel knowing that you didn't quit when the shiz hit the fan?

Refer back to this section when things are going tough. Read your answers over and over until they are burned in your brain. Copy your answers on Post-It Notes and plaster them all around your house. Do whatever you need to do to keep your head in the game.

"Failure is an option, quitting is not." You can learn from failure, but you won't learn a darn thing if you quit!

Failure is an option, quitting is not.

Let's Wrap It Up

✔ Be a risk-taker. Hardship is better than regret.

✔ Do the work. But if you must work to the bone, do it with passion.

✔ Do something every single day to help achieve your dream, even if you don't feel like it.

✔ Failure is an option. Quitting is not. You can learn a lot from failure, but you can't learn anything from quitting.

Notes:

_____

_____

_____

_____

_____

_____

The Secret to Success – Your F.I.R.E. Team

"A friend is someone who understands your past, believes in your future, and accepts you just the way you are."
— Anonymous

"No, You Can't Do It All On Your Own"

Although you can, as the saying goes, "Do anything you set your mind to," someone really should have revised that statement to read, "You can do anything you set your mind to if you are willing to ask for and accept help when needed. Whether they knew it or not, every successful person achieved success because someone was in their corner backing them up. It's great to be independent and to have a can-do attitude, but be sure not to deceive yourself into thinking you'll never need anyone's help along the way. That's a surefire way to sabotage your success. As I said before, one of the biggest dream killers is ego. If you allow your pride to get in your way when it comes to asking for help, you might as well just stop reading this book and forget about pursuing your dream. There is an old proverb that says, "Pride goes before the fall." Don't let your ego trip you up. Okay, it's workout time! Answer the following 3 juicy questions with a straight and honest heart.

On a scale of 1 to 10, one being easy and ten being extremely difficult, how hard is it for you to ask for help?

How has not asking for help stunted your success?

What lies do you tell yourself about asking for help? (Hint: Often clients might say, *"I feel like a failure when I ask for help."* Or, *"I am managing just fine on my own."*)

Accept that help is a useful and necessary aspect of success.

Stop listening to the lies and letting ego stand in your way. If your friend needed help wouldn't you want to help them? I know you would. Well guess what? Your friends want to help you too. Let them! *"Accept that help is a useful and necessary aspect of success."*

"The Company You Keep"

While going it alone is a great way to set yourself up for failure, so is hanging with the wrong crowd. One of the harsh realities of the world is that people will often judge you based on the company you keep. Who are the people surrounding you? What are they into? Are they productive members of the community? Are they positive and uplifting? Or are they bitter, jealous, angry and negative? Do they show up ready to lend a helping hand – or ready to tear someone down? It may be a bit difficult to conduct this mental performance review of your friends, but it's necessary because, as the mantra goes, *"You are the average of the 5 people you spend the most time with."* You've got to know exactly whose company you're keeping and what effect they may be having on you and your success. Take inventory of your friend warehouse. You might come to the conclusion that you need to trim the fat, but that may not be such a bad idea. We'll go into more detail on that later.

"Squad Ability And F.I.R.E. Teams"

The Marine Corps is a highly effective and successful organization that gets results. There are lots of lessons to be learned from the Corps, so let's get to it. In boot camp, recruits are separated into squad ability groups for physical training. Why do they do this? Why wouldn't they just let all the recruits work out together all at once? Because the kids would get hurt, that's why. Instead, the recruits are strategically placed in groups that challenge them without killing them. In the process, everyone improves because the strongest kid in the group doesn't want to lose his spot as the "strongest" kid and the weakest kid wants to catch up to the strongest. They are each motivating and encouraging one another to do better.

The Corps also divides personnel down into fire teams. These teams originated way back when. I won't bore you with the history behind it all, but the bottom line is these teams were created to maximize efficiency on the battlefield. Success is much like a battle. You've got to fight for your life, you've got to give it your all and push as hard as you can to come out victoriously. This is no easy feat all on your own. You need your very own fire team. But not the kind created by the Marine Corps...

Your F.I.R.E. team must be comprised of **F**abulous friends who are **I**nspiring, **R**eliable and **E**ager to see you succeed. These people continuously lift you up. They are your number one fans; your biggest cheerleaders. They are there to help you at a moment's notice and genuinely want to see you do well. Of course not every friend you have will earn a spot on your F.I.R.E. team – that's okay. You don't need a gang of peeps, you just need a few solid friends who have your back. Remember how I had you take inventory of your friendship warehouse in the last section? What did you conclude? Hopefully, by now you have a good idea of who falls into your "I should probably cut you out" list and who falls into your "I need you on my F.I.R.E. team list." If not, go back and start making a note of who belongs in which group. In the space below, list three or four friends you know would make an excellent addition to your F.I.R.E. team and what kind of support you feel they give you. Are they motivators, helping hands, good listeners? Beside their name, list the best way they consistently show up for you:

_____
_____
_____
_____
_____

The next step is to reach out and contact the people you listed above. Share with them the goal or dream you are currently pursuing. Ask them if they are on board to support you in this journey. Be upfront and honest with them. Let them know you'd be honored if they would be a part of your F.I.R.E. team. Don't be discouraged if it just so happens that a friend or two decline your invitation. Consider it a victory because you need *fabulous* friends on your F.I.R.E. team and clearly this person wasn't fabulous! Keep it moving to the next person until you find the right people. Once you assemble your F.I.R.E. team you'll be unstoppable.

"It's A Two-Way Street"

This may seem like a no-brainer, but friendship is a two-way street. When we get focused on our path, sometimes it can be really easy to forget to pull our weight in the friendship department. Just like you're depending on your F.I.R.E. team, remember that you are also a team member for someone else. If you want them to show up for you, you've got to show up for them. As you begin tackling projects and tasks, don't forget to schedule time in for phone calls, lunches, dinners or even Skype dates with your friends. Heck, why not schedule

Remember to give generously (and cheerfully) of your time and talents.

monthly F.I.R.E. Power Parties with your friends where you come together, kick it and celebrate one another. But remember to share the focus on them and the things going on in their lives rather than make your time of fellowship all about you and your dreams. Success is about give and take, and paying it forward. *"Remember to give generously (and cheerfully) of your time and talents."* Success won't be too far behind.

"Make It A Mastermind"

Another great approach to creating an amazing support system is to consider joining a mastermind group. The mastermind is a concept first introduced by Napoleon Hill in his book *Think and Grow Rich*. Hill describes the mastermind as, "coordination of knowledge and effort, in a spirit of harmony, between two or more people, for the attainment of a definite purpose."[5] In plain English, a mastermind, usually 4-6 people but sometimes up to 10, is a group that gets together for the purpose of achieving a common goal. It's important to recognize the difference between your F.I.R.E. team and a mastermind group. Your F.I.R.E. team will most likely be made up of family and friends who are interested in helping you fulfill your dream but who do not necessarily share your dream. Your mastermind group will be comprised of individuals who are at a similar level as you and who are trying to achieve a similar goal. If, for example, you're a budding entrepreneur, the members of your group would consist of other aspiring entrepreneurs. If you're a health enthusiast, your mastermind group might be comprised of fitness instructors and health conscious individuals who want to create a thinner nation. See how it works?

To be fair, you must be warned that being part of a mastermind group is a big responsibility. It's definitely not for the half-assers of the world. If you're a commitment-phobe, this might not be the way for you to go, either. A mastermind group is for those who are serious about reaching the

5   Think and Grow Rich, Napoleon Hill p. 251

next level. It's not for everyone, so don't be discouraged if you aren't sure this is a viable option for you. If, on the other hand, you feel you're ready to do whatever it takes to achieve your dreams, then I definitely recommend you get involved ASAP.

Mastermind groups typically meet once a month, though some groups choose to meet more frequently. Each person is expected to participate, contribute and be fully present. The benefits far outweigh the time you spend with your group. In fact, most people can't get enough of their mastermind group. Together you create a think tank of ideas, share what works and what doesn't, network, pool resources, provide accountability, and give one another valuable feedback. This is by no means an all-inclusive list of the benefits you'll get from a mastermind group, but it does give you a good idea of what you'd get out of being part of one.

Mastermind Group Success Tips:

1. Do your research.
Don't just throw your dollar bills at the first program you see. Ask to speak with people who have previously been in the mastermind and hear what they have to say. Make sure the program you choose caters to people in your situation.

2. Choose a fee-based group that won't be a financial burden.
Financially investing in a mastermind group will help keep you more focused and accountable. On the flip side, investing in a program that far exceeds your income will create a burden, not only financially but also emotionally. Ultimately you won't be able to do your best work because you'll be resentful of the cost. So choose wisely.

> *3. Be fully present, participate and do the work.*
> You get out of the group what you put into it. Free yourself of distractions and make your group a true priority. Enough said.

The cost of a mastermind program varies greatly. You can find them anywhere from free all the way up to $20,000+. That's quite the pretty penny, right? Of course, I'm not suggesting you go out and drop twenty grand. I'm simply suggesting you do some research and find the facilitator and program that speaks to you. That being said, I can't leave you without offering up my personal theory on the money factor when it comes to mastermind groups. So here it is: invest in a group that charges a fee. It doesn't have to be a 5-figure investment, but you should definitely have a financial stake in the group. "*When people invest their hard earned cash, they have a tendency to be more committed.*" It's not a theory, it's a fact.

When people invest their hard earned cash, they have a tendency to be more committed.

Let's Wrap It Up

- ✔ Success is not achieved alone.

- ✔ Ego is a dream killer.

- ✔ Your F.I.R.E. team consists of:
  Fabulous friends who are
  Inspiring
  Reliable and
  Eager to see you succeed!

- ✔ Friendship is a two-way street. Always give generously (and cheerfully) of your time and talents.

- ✔ Join a fee-based mastermind group to help you soar to the top.

Notes:

_____
_____
_____
_____
_____
_____

✥

So Many Dreams, So Little Time

"It may be that those who do most, dream most."
- Stephen Butler Leacock

"The Multi-Passionate Dreamer"

By now you've probably had about 40,000 different thoughts running around in your head as you contemplate how you're going to make your dream come true. But there's one thing we haven't really touched on. What to do when you have more than one dream? What do you do when you are multi-passionate? Do you pick the one you love most and forget the rest? What if you love them all equally, and for different reasons? The answer is: you follow all of your dreams and work towards fulfilling each and every one. *"But Rachel, that's impossible. I can barely make one dream come true, let alone 4 or 5,"* you may be thinking to yourself. Not so my friend. *"You can work on several goals and achieve each one if you strategize*

You can work on several goals and achieve each one if you strategize and plan it out the right way.

and plan it out the right way." Think of it as multi-tasking your dreams. The key element is focus. You must focus, then divide, then conquer.

"Finding and Keeping Your Focus"

Being passionate about more than one life path can be very confusing, frustrating and at times overwhelming. Inevitably, once you start heading towards your goal you'll find that everything seems to become a distraction. That's why learning how to find and keep your focus is of the utmost importance. There are boatloads of strategies and philosophies out there to help you find your focus, but I'm going to share four of my favorites with you. These are effective and have a proven tack record not only in my life, but for many of my clients as well.

Focus Strategy #1: The Brain Dump

This is hands down my favorite way to get focused. A brain dump is simply writing down every idea you have and action step you need to take in order to achieve your goal. You can do this activity on a sheet of paper, or you can get really creative and make a visual board. I prefer to use a board because I'm a visual person, but I also provide a photo of what a brain dump can look like on paper.

To create your brain dump board, you'll need a poster board, a pen or pencil, and a pack of Post-It® notes. Section your board off into three sections: to-do, in-progress, and completed. Set a timer for 10 minutes and in that time jot down as many thoughts and ideas – that pertain to your goal – as you can on individual Post-it® notes. As I mentioned before, you can also write down your list on a sheet of paper, but if you decide to go that route, make sure you number each idea. Since I learned to do this exercise using Post-it® notes, that's the method I prefer. But tomato, tomahto.

Once time is up, review your ideas and see if any of them can be grouped together to form a category. Next, you'll move all your Post-It® notes under the appropriate category. Easy enough, right? Well, we're not done just yet. It's great to have your ideas categorized, but now you need to write down the action steps you're going to take for each idea. Be as detailed as possible. The more action steps you have, the better. Finally, categorize and put your action steps, aka your to-do list, in order of priority.

The reason I love this system is because although it requires some time putting it all together, once you're done you'll have everything neatly organized. As you start doing things on your lists, using the Post-It® system, you can start moving your notes to the "in progress" or "completed" section. If you're doing a brain dump on paper, you can annotate the action steps with a "P," as "in progress" or cross them off completely once you're done. Let me tell you, it feels *great* to start moving your notes over and seeing the left side of that board get empty. Before you know it, everything will be done and you'll be well on your way to mission accomplishment!

If you're feeling a little confused, don't be. I've created an easy-to-follow instructional video showing you exactly how to create a brain dump board on my site, www.thetailormadelife.com, in the bonus book section. You'll also get to see what my board looks like.

The following picture is an example of what this exercise might look like on a sheet of paper for a blogger wanting to get more notoriety and transition over to become a published author. Note: This isn't an all-inclusive example. In real life, there might be a writing plan in the to-do list for the book-writing task, and many other steps.

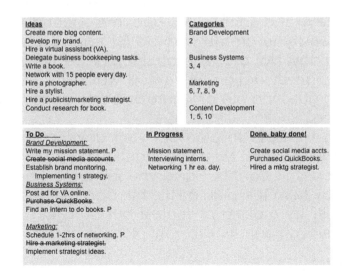

Remember to have fun with this activity and revisit your board or list on a daily basis. The goal is to take as much action as possible each and every day.

Focus Strategy #2: Plan, plan, and plan.

Plan your day, week, month and year. I can hear my dad's voice in the background harping away, *"If you fail to plan, you plan to fail."* True indeed! Planning each day gives you a purpose and helps you take your productivity to the next level. In the book *EntreLeadership,* financial guru and NY Times Best-Selling Author Dave Ramsey writes, "Strange as it may seem, when you work a daily plan in pursuit of your written goals that flow from your mission statement born of your vision for living your dreams, you are energized after a tough, long day." And that's truer than true!

It may take a little bit of effort in the beginning to get in the habit of planning your day, week, month and year, but I assure you, it's well-worth the effort. In order to effectively plan your year, as we mentioned before, you have to have the end in mind. Identify your main priority and go from there. What steps do you need to take each month to make your vision a reality? Then break it down by week, then by day. Start out with 5 or 10 minutes a day, and soon it will become second nature. I recommend you create a to-do list each night for the following day. Not only will you sleep better knowing you have a plan of action when you wake up, but it also takes the guessing out of where to begin once your day gets going.

Taking the time to plan out your day increases your productivity by 20%. Most importantly, stick to the schedule as best you can, but give yourself some slack if you veer away from the plan a little bit. Don't forget to have fun with it! Try making a contest out of it and see how many days you can stick to your plan. Or better yet, have one of your F.I.R.E. team members hold you accountable to write your plan each day!

Focus Strategy #3: De-Clutter Your Station.

Have you ever tried working in a chaotic environment? How did that work out for you? I'll venture to say it probably didn't go so well. Sure, you may have completed the task, but I'm pretty sure your clarity and mental focus were tested on more than one occasion. This is because the brain cannot focus amidst clutter and disorganization. Even for those of us who insist our "controlled chaos system" works, the truth is, establishing order and organization make us all much more effective and productive.

Take a good look at your surroundings. Are you working in a hot mess? If so, you need to take action immediately, if not sooner. Set aside an hour a day and start cleaning and organizing. Better yet, if you can swing it, take an entire day or weekend to de-clutter. If you *really* have a "hot mess situation," consider asking one or two members of your F.I.R.E. team to lend a helping hand or consider hiring a professional organizer. I guarantee that once you have an organized environment you'll immediately feel more focused. While writing this book, I took an entire weekend to redo our bathroom, living room and my home office. The result? Well, you're reading this book, so it obviously helped improve my focus and productivity in finishing it. Not to mention, I now have beautifully decorated areas in my home. Everyone wins, I got more productive, and my guests feel more welcome in my home. Your turn – give it a try!

Focus Strategy #4: Get Self-Control.

When all else fails, you can always get Self-Control. No, seriously, download the computer program called Self-Control. I don't know about you, but I could get lost for endless hours surfing the web – "hanging out" – with my friends on Facebook, following my favorite celebs on Twitter and otherwise wasting my day away. In fact, many of these activities account for the significant delay of completing this very book. That is, until I discovered Self-Control. It's a free, downloadable program that allows you to create a "black" list of websites that can be blocked for a specific amount of time. The great thing about the program, is that once you set it, there's no way to unset it. You can't shut down your computer or even uninstall the program (I've tried). You literally have to wait until time runs out before you can access the sites on your black list. This program is incredibly helpful for increasing focus and productivity, *trust me*. Google it!

There you have it. Four no-bull strategies for finding and keeping your focus. Don't feel pressured to implement them all at once, or even at all. Just try one at a time until you find the one that works for you. I have personally used each of these strategies at one point or another and have found them to be really helpful to stay in alignment with my vision and mission, and to ultimately achieve my goals.

"Tying It All Together"

One of the questions I often hear from my multi-passion-ate peeps is, *"How do I tie it all together?"* How can you tie in all your dreams when they are all so unique? The answer to that question isn't necessarily clean-cut and straightfor-ward. Some dreams can be easily intertwined even if they seem polar opposites at first glance. For example, I know a brilliant woman who had a successful career in educa-tion and earned a higher education degree in culinary nu-trition. That seems pretty straightforward, right? Teaching is teaching, even if the subject matter changes. As she grew her culinary nutrition practice, she developed a passion for business marketing. Now we're starting to draw outside the lines a bit. Teaching, nutrition, food and business market-ing? Would you think those could work together? Well, she did. Today she runs an amazing business where she not only teaches people how to develop better relationships with food but also offers her services as a marketing strategist. All this from one website!

I know another cool chick that has a burning passion for yoga, jewelry and history. How the heck could she combine all three and make an honest living? She does it by creating custom jewelry, teaching classes, and offering consultations. Of course, this is an entrepreneurial venture, but the bottom line is she is multi-passionate and has found a way to follow and achieve her dreams. You can, too!

Those are two examples of women taking totally different dreams and seamlessly tying them all together. Now of course, there are times when your two dreams won't mesh as well. That's when cross promotion comes into play. My mentor, Marie Forleo (yes I'm mentioning her again 'cause she's that freakin' fab!), is not only a brilliant businesswoman, but she's also quite the fly girl when it comes to shaking her groove thang. By the way, I first heard the term 'multi-passionate' from Marie, so props to her for putting to words a feeling many of us have experienced. The avid dancer and music lover that she is, Marie parlayed her passions into a successful career as an MTV Hip-Hop Choreographer/Producer/Dance Instructor. But she didn't stop there. Also having a passion for helping others, Marie built a million dollar business teaching women entrepreneurs how to live Rich, Happy and Hot® with programs such as Rich, Happy, Hot Live; Rich, Happy, Hot B-School (from which yours truly, moi, am a graduate) and her renowned Adventure Mastermind Program. Did I mention that she has also written a book that is now published in over 9 languages? How was she able to follow her dreams and have it all? There was no magic formula. She just did, and continues to do, what she loves to do and cross-promotes the heck out of herself.

I know the examples I've shared depict an entrepreneurial approach, but being a multi-passionate dreamer doesn't mean you have to find a way to monetize or create careers out of all your dreams. You can focus on fulfilling on one dream career while you achieve your other dreams by engaging in them as hobbies. For example, I always thought I wanted to be a famous actress or dancer. Turns out I didn't have the passion or drive for the craft of acting to invest the time and energy one needs to have if that's their dream. I did enjoy being center stage, though, so I translated the love for being in front of an audience to public speaking. Either way, I'm still fulfilling my dream of being in the spotlight. The ways you choose to pursue your dreams are up to you. Whatever street you take to get there, just remember, you don't have to choose. **You can fulfill *all* your dreams in one way, shape or form.**

"*You can fulfill all your dreams in one way, shape or form.*"

It's exercise time! List all of your dreams. And when I say all, I mean *all*, not just the one or two you think you might pursue.

_____
_____
_____
_____
_____
_____

Which ones do you want to pursue for financial gain? Are there any you can tie in together? Which ones will you focus on as hobbies? Take the time to really think about this exercise because as you start to develop your plan, this will help you stay focused and on target.

Let's Wrap It Up

✔ You can work on several goals and achieve each one if you strategize and plan it out the right way.

✔ Utilize the four focus strategies to stay on track and become a multi-passionate dream achiever.

✔ You can fulfill *all* your dreams in one way, shape or form. You just have to decide which ones will be for money and which ones will be for love and which ones will be for both!

Notes:

_____

_____

_____

_____

_____

_____

❧

Funding Your Life

*"Let us more and more insist on raising funds of
love, of kindness, of understanding, of peace.
The rest will be given."*
                              - Mother Teresa of Calcutta

*"If I had more _ _ _ _ _ _ _ _ _ _ then everything
would be better."*

Do you ever think that if you had more money then
your life would be better? If you had a bigger house,
you'd feel better? If you had a new car, fancy clothes
or a high-powered career, life would be much better?
Of course you've thought
those things – we all have.
But we were and still are
wrong! Nothing could be
further from the truth. *"Having more things doesn't
make your life better; it just*

**Having more things
doesn't make your life
better; it just makes it
full, of well, more things.**

makes it full, of well, more things." Rich people are not
necessarily happier. Yes, they *seem* happier and they do
get to take bigger, better, longer vacations than the rest
of us. But you and I both know they have their own crap-
sandwich of problems.

Now, I'm not suggesting you stop aspiring to create
a life of wealth and abundance. Never that. I'm telling
you not to let yourself fall into the trap of thinking and/or
obsessing that more of *anything* in your life would magi-
cally, deliciously make everything in your world fall into

place. It won't. In fact, if you won the lotto tomorrow, you'd probably have more problems than today because everyone and their mother would be coming out of the woods asking for a handout. Or, someone might come knocking on your door with court papers trying to sue you for their cut. Just ask Bethenny Frankel, the Bravo TV star of several shows, most recently "Bethenny Ever After" and the creator of the SkinnyGirl brand that includes the SkinnyGirl Margarita. Recently Ms. Frankel sold her SkinnyGirl Brand of pre-mixed cocktails to Beam Global aka Jim Beam for a reported $100+ million dollars Chu-ching! Right? Wrong! Shortly after the news broke, guess who came knocking on Ms. Frankel's door asking for their cut? Yup, her former management company. Rumors say the management company wants $100 million dollars and now, while she should be shopping her little heart out and rolling around naked on hundred dollars bills, Bethenny is dealing with lawyers and the headache of trying to protect her assets. In the infamous words of fallen rap artist, The Notorious B.I.G., "Mo' money, mo' problems."

As we go further into this chapter, we're going to get a little woo-woo and talk about our life's purpose as well as delve into the feelings associated with money. But don't worry, because we're also going to get into the nitty-gritty details of how to finance your dreams.

"The Purpose of Life."

In 1961 John F. Kennedy said in his speech, "Ask not what your country can do for you – ask what you can do for your country." I've always loved

"The purpose of life is to matter, to be productive, to be useful, to have it make some difference that you have lived at all."

that quote because there is something so powerful in being a servant for others. Are you a positive contributor to society? What will your legacy be? How do you want to be remembered? True success isn't just about material wealth – it's about being a successful person, helping others and giving generously. Leo Rosten said, *"The purpose of life is to matter, to be productive, to be useful, to have it make some difference that you have lived at all."*

There you have it. You've spent years wondering the purpose of life and it only took eight chapters before I gave you the answer. You're welcome! Okay, okay, I'm just teasing. But to get serious for a moment, when you look at the big picture of your life, what matters most? Don't make chasing the paper your priority because despite popular opinion, success and wealth are not synonymous. You have gifts and talents that will make you successful far beyond the dollars. All that being said, we do still need to talk about money, why you need it and how you can get some. So away we go.

"It's all about the Benjamins, Yo!"

There's no doubt in my mind you are committed to fulfilling your dreams and having it all. After all, you took the initiative to pick up and read this book. But what happens when you achieve success and yes, even wealth? Will you be able to handle it? Let's find out by examining your relationship with money and your current financial situation. How do you feel about you finances right now, today? Do you feel good, bad or indifferent? Do you feel satisfied? Do you have enough to cover your basic needs and still put a few dollars away for savings and retirement? Are you struggling to make ends meet, living paycheck to paycheck? Do you find yourself getting stressed at the end of the month because you're down to your last $5 bill? Are you comfortable but still not quite where you'd like to be?

I've felt every single one of those emotions. I've lived paycheck to paycheck. I've been in line at the grocery store holding my breath just hoping the card would go through. I've had to turn down lunch with friends because

I couldn't even pull a $20 out of the ATM. I was once that girl who would avoid opening bills just so I wouldn't have to face the music. At 26 years old, I was over $40,000 in debt even though I had no children, and made well over $60,000 a year. The problem was a combination of poor money management, a negative relationship with money and of course, my constant desire to keep up with "The Joneses." When I finally asked myself the questions I'm about to ask you in the Money Matters Q&A Session, things began to change. In less than three years, I became completely debt-free. I was able to purchase two vehicles in cash – one brand new and one used, I furnished our entire home and still had three months worth of savings in the bank. Was it easy? Heck no! It took hardcore commitment. Was it worth it? Darn skippy it was! Today, I only buy if I have the cash in the bank. How did I do it? After asking myself those tough questions, I read every book I could find on money management and then I started implementing the best concepts. My two favorite finance gurus are Suze Orman and Dave Ramsey. I also like David Bach and Robert and Kim Kiyosaki. You'll find a list of my favorite finance books on my site, www.the-tailormadelife.com in the bonus book section. I've also posted some great supplemental worksheets for you to download.

"The Money Matters Q+A Session"

How you *feel* about and *view* money plays an important factor in your success. Those who constantly perceive themselves as 'have-nots' often have not. The following are some questions for you to meditate on. You don't necessarily have to write down answers, but definitely marinate on these questions. You may be surprised as you discover your true sentiments on money.

Soul Searching on Money Matters

1. What is my personal attitude when it comes to money? (Many people have thoughts such as, *"I'll never be rich." "I'm happy to live on a little." "I love money and want more!"*)
2. What is my money personality? Am I a spender, saver or risk-taker?
3. What are my feelings/thoughts towards people *with* money?
   (Hint: Some might think, *"They're better than me." "They should pay higher taxes." "I need to follow their lead."*)
4. What are my feelings/thoughts towards people *without* money?
   (Hint: *"They did it to themselves." "I wish I could do more to help them."*
5. How much money is okay for me to want in my life?
   (Often people feel guilty for wanting money. Think about how you feel about your financial ambitions.)
6. How do I feel about giving to others?
7. Do I recognize if and when I am being selfish with my money?
8. Do I have any deep-rooted fears associated with money?
   (i.e. *"I'm afraid to spend." "I'm afraid to save and never fully live my life."*)
9. Do I feel good about my current money situation?

Now that we've gotten the deep down, soul-searching, woo-woo stuff out of the way, let's talk straight numbers.

This time I do want you to write the numbers down. Putting numbers on paper helps make them real and therefore helps make your dream become a real, achievable goal. Be very specific. Don't round off or give ballpark answers.

How much money do I have? (Be specific. Don't put how much you *think* you have. Take a minute or two to look up your bank account info and write down the actual amount you have.)

How much debt do I have? (Again, be specific. No rounding off. Write it down to the penny.)

How much money do I need to cover my basic expenses?

How much do I earn per hour, week, month, and year?

Do I have a specific amount of money I want to have in this lifetime? If so, how much?

These numbers along with your FICO score are tremendously important because then and only then will you be able to determine your financial goals and potential. In case you aren't familiar, your FICO score is your credit rating and it makes or breaks you when it comes time to buying big ticket items like a house, a car or even applying for a loan to finance your business. By law, you are entitled to one free copy of your credit report. Take advantage of this freebie. You can also subscribe to services that monitor your FICO score and alert you of any changes. I found this service really helpful when I was working on paying down my debt. It's really rewarding to see your score go up as your debt goes down. I definitely recommend you look into it.

"The B-Word"

It's time to talk about the B-word. BUDGET. John Maxwell says, *"A budget is you telling your money where to go instead of wondering where it went."* True indeed, Mr. Maxwell, true indeed. I know many of us have wondered on more than one occasion, *"Dang, where did my money go?"* In fact,

> **"A budget is you telling your money where to go instead of wondering where it went."**

when I returned home from Iraq in 2003 I had saved $20,000 but by 2005 I didn't have a dime of that money left over. I didn't have anything to show for it except for better vision since I had spent $3,000 on Lasik surgery. Worst of all, I was still in the hole $40,000. To this day, I still ask myself, *"Where did that twenty grand go?"* This is the reason I'm a big believer in the budget system. Your mission, should you choose to accept it (and you better choose to accept it, shoo!) is to create your budget right now. Don't wait until tomorrow because as my father always said, tomorrow never comes. If you've never done a budget before don't worry, you know your girl has the hookup. Head over to www.thetailormadelife.com and use the fillable Budget Worksheet pdf. Remember to be realistic when you create your budget and leave some cushion space for each entry. Please don't write $100 in the eating out category for the month if you know darn well that's how much you might spend on one outing. In case you're wondering why I'm having you do your budget now, let me ask you this, *"If not now, when?"*

Success Tips for Budgeting:

1. Take the time.
Don't brush off creating a budget. If you've heard it all before but aren't working with a budget, then guess what? You need to hear it again and this time, take action!

2. Cut yourself some slack.
It takes time to get into the habit of budgeting, so don't be discouraged if you fall off a day or two. Just stick with it.

3. Give yourself some cushion.
Especially in the food category, be sure to overestimate just a little bit. We often take for granted how much we actually consume.

4. Team work makes a dream work.
If you have a partner, make sure you both work on the budget together so everyone is on the same page as to how the funds are going to be allocated.

With your personal budget beautifully executed, we can now move onto creating a fabulous plan to fund your life. One thing many of us tend to overlook when we're pursuing our dreams is how much money we need and how much we're capable of earning. If your dream involves a new career path, you're definitely going to need a nest egg. If your dream is to be an entrepreneur, then you *definitely* need to put a solid financial structure in place. Not having a plan will leave you constantly focusing on money, wondering if you have enough and where more will come from. This vicious cycle of constant worry is an energy zapper and it takes your focus away from pursuing your heart's desire. Seriously, do not continue reading until you've completed your budget.

"Savvy Spending"

Just as soon as you start pursuing your dream and get your finances in order, you'll notice enticing ads will start popping up all around you. You'll be tempted to spend or "invest" your hard earned money in yourself and your dream. Warning: don't say yes to every single miracle product or service under the sun that claims to help you fulfill your dream. Believe me, I know how tempting it can be to spend $47 here and $97 there. The problem with a little here and a little there is that it all adds up, and it adds up quickly. Next thing you know you've spent several thousands of dollars. Before you drop even one single dollar on a product or service, get informed. Do a cost analysis on *everything* and shop around. See how much other people are charging for the same or similar product/service. Compare the quality, timeliness and overall nature of the offer and definitely read reviews. Ask yourself, *"Do I want, need or must have this in order to succeed?"* Like your budget, this exercise takes a little bit of time but if you don't put in the work upfront, you will pay down the road both figuratively and literally. And since there's no time like the present, let's go ahead and make a list of your wants, needs and must haves. What do you need to spend money on in order to achieve your dream? Do you need a particular degree or certification? Do you need a website, headshots, or marketing campaign? Do you need a coach or trainer? Could your dream benefit from you hiring a housekeeper to help you free up your time so you can focus on doing the important work versus vacuuming the house? Really stretch your thought process and think outside of the box. Use the space below to compile your list. Try to make it as all-inclusive as possible and be sure to write the cost next to each item.

If I didn't provide enough space, break out a piece of paper and keep adding to the list. Once your list is on paper, you'll be able to have a clear sense of which items are priorities and which ones can wait. Having the dollar value next to the items on your list will help you know exactly how much you need to make your **don't rush to spend your money on things you think you need until you've done your homework.** dream happen. And remember, "*don't rush to spend your money on things you think you need until you've done your homework.*"

"Creative Earning"

You did your budget, right? If not, stop everything and do your budget *right now*. Okay, good. You've done the work and we can now move forward. With your budget in place, clear knowledge of how much money you need and want, and how much financing your dream will cost (per the list you just created in the previous section) you can now figure out pretty much down to the penny how much money you need to earn to fund your dream.

If you work in a traditional environment, you're probably limited in how you can increase your earnings. You may have the option to negotiate a higher salary or ask for overtime hours, but aside from that, what you make is what you make. This is when you need to get creative and start thinking out of the box to create multiple streams of income.

Refer back to your list of needs, wants and must haves and determine which are your first priorities. Do some number crunching and calculate how much additional income you need to move forward with these purchases. Whenever I ask my clients to do a number crunch, there's a lot of hesitation and sometimes a little confusion. Let me give you an example to show you my interpretation of number crunching.

Let's pretend you earn $3,000 per month and have monthly expenses totaling $2,800. That only leaves you $200 each month for whatever. Now let's suppose the first priority on your list of 'dream expenses' is a $1,000 certification program. With the disposable $200 you have each month, that means you'd have to save that surplus for 5 months before you can enroll for your program. But of course, you don't want to start in 5 months; you want to start in 2 months. That means you need to find a way to earn an extra $300 per month or roughly an extra $10 per day each month. Figuring out how to make an extra $10 per day sounds pretty manageable, doesn't it? This method of number crunching is so elementary, and yet, people don't take the time to go through the list and do the work. Don't let this be you. Take the time, do the work.

This section is titled "creative earning," so let's talk about some ways to increase your cash flow. I first recommend you review your budget and see where you can cut some corners. Even a simple step like packing your lunch once or twice a week can save you about $80 per month. Using coupons, shopping sales and unplugging your electrical appliances when you're not using them are also great ways to add another $20-$50 in savings a month. Of course you can always take a look around the house and start selling items you no longer use. Prior to moving to Japan, I did a sale of my own and raised over $1,000. You'd be surprised how many items you have in your home that will add to your bottom line. Check out www.bookoo.com to find a virtual yard sale near you. It's one of my favorite resources.

Some other ways to earn a little extra cash might include taking on a part-time job or looking for freelance jobs on places like odesk.com, elance.com and hiremymom.com to name a few. If you're a crafty person, you might consider selling your creations on etsy.com. On MSN Money, one person reported earning $20 to $120 per month by selling on Etsy. Not bad for doing something you already love to do, right? These are just a few examples to get you started, but it's not an all-inclusive list. I'm pretty sure there are at least a dozen other ways you can scrape up a few extra bucks each month to start checking things off your list. If you really want to make your dreams a reality, you'll find the way to raise the money. Necessity is the mother of invention. Now it's time for *you* to get creative and list a few ways you can earn some extra cashola. Getting creative and thinking outside the box will get you one dollar closer to your dream.

_____

_____

_____

_____

_____

Life is not meant to be all about the Benjamin's, but the reality is that money is a necessary part of life and sometimes a very necessary component to help us achieve our dreams. Really take the time to do the work in this chapter. When it comes to funding your life, it takes time, patience, dedication and sacrifice. But trust me, it's all worth it in the end. Oh, and by the way, if you're an aspiring entrepreneur, I highly recommend you pick up a copy of Carol Roth's bestseller *The Entrepreneur Equation*. She really goes over the nitty gritty numbers of building a business.

Let's Wrap It Up

- ✓ Having more things, doesn't make your life better, it just makes it full of well – more things.

- ✓ "A budget is you telling your money where to go instead of wondering where it went."

- ✓ The purpose of life is to matter, to be productive, to be useful, to have it make some difference that you have lived at all.

- ✓ Don't rush to spend your money on things you think you need until you've done your homework.

- ✓ Get creative and think outside of the box when it comes to generating multiple streams of income.

Notes:

_____
_____
_____
_____
_____
_____

❦

Seven Secrets to Red Hot Success

*"Success comes to those who have proceeded to do
what the rest of us have always intended to do."*
— Anonymous

`#1. Be Inspired`

Inspiration comes from many different places and, like
love, is often found when you least expect it. The inspiration
for the title of this book came to me while I was cooking dinner. Such an ordinary task, one I do each evening, yet there
it was like a bolt of lighting – the title of my first book. That
one moment birthed an amazing transformation in my life.
Not only did my focus increase like never before, but for the
next nine months I was filled with the amazing by-products
of inspiration – hope, excitement, fulfillment, peace, and
joy.

Inspiration allows you to envision yourself doing the
amazing things you've always dreamed of doing. It lights
you up and enables you to move forward towards achieving your goals. When you're inspired, you are able to live
as you've always intended. Strive to be inspired each and
every single day and you'll have a life filled with happiness,
hopefulness and ultimately success.

`#2. Put Yourself on Display`

No one will know who you are or what you're capable
of achieving if you don't put yourself and your talents on
display. *"The most successful people are those who are
willing to put themselves out there and who are open to*

receiving both praise and criticism." Take the center stage of your life and don't be afraid to let the world know just who and how special

The most successful people are those who are willing to put themselves out there and who are open to receiving both praise and criticism.

you are! I'm serious! This is a non-negotiable. Your success is contingent upon your ability to show others what you can do. So get out there, get on display and show the world who they're dealing with.

"#3. Stop Searching for Instant Gratification"

Meryl Streep once said, *"Instant gratification is not soon enough."* Boy, do I know that feeling. I'm sure you've felt it, too. The sensation that no matter what you do, the results you want are just not happening fast enough. Why does this bother us so much? The fact of the matter is that we've grown accustomed to instant gratification. We are, as the Grammy Award-winning group The Black Eyed Peas wrote, *"the now generation."* In this age of modern technology, we are used to having instant access to just about everything. We carry smart phones which allow us to call, email, listen to music, play games and do just about anything else with the swipe of a finger. Search engines like Google make finding out anything about anything easier than ever. And they continue to work on making it even easier. Before the inception of Google Instant, the average web search took about 25 seconds: nine seconds to type it, less than one second for Google to return a result and 15 seconds to pick the best result. Google Instant shaved two to five seconds off of that time.[6] It's no wonder we all crave instant gratification, we've become desensitized to the notion of waiting.

Heed my warning – stop searching for instant gratification. Success takes time so stop focusing on making things

6   http://articles.cnn.com/2010-09-08/tech/google.search_1_results-pages-google-search-giant?_s=PM:TECH

happen fast. Just focus on making things *happen*. Practice patience, and by that, I mean take
your time and be strategic in the

You don't have to be complacent to be patient.

decisions you make. Keep working on doing all that you
can to make your dream come true, but don't worry about
how fast or slow things are happening. *"You don't have to
be complacent to be patient."* Just keep doing and know
that your time is coming.

"#4. Remember Overnight Success Doesn't Happen Overnight"

Do you remember when Justin Bieber first hit the scene
and everyone caught a case of "Bieber Fever?" Well,
mostly everyone. I didn't join the fan bandwagon until
a year or two later. But to the rest of the world, seem-
ingly overnight, this kid became a success and had everyone singing, *Baby, baby, baby*. Is that how it really
happened? Did Justin post his video on YouTube on a
Monday morning and achieve international stardom on
Tuesday? No! Of course not. C'mon, that's not how the
real world operates. Yes, Justin Bieber did get discovered after posting a video of himself on YouTube, but
his mega success *did not* happen overnight. I won't ruin
the story for you, but his
biopic concert movie
Never Say Never gives
you the real deal story on
the setbacks, the frustrations and the time it took

Real, lasting success takes time, hard work, energy, dedication, commitment and perseverance.

from when Scooter Braun first clicked on Bieber's video
to his first sold-out concert. The bottom line is: Don't believe the hype. *"Real, lasting success takes time, hard
work, energy, dedication, commitment and perseverance."* To quote Dave Ramsey, *"I worked my butt off for
15 years and then became an overnight success."* Keep

your focus and momentum going and before you know it, you'll be an overnight success yourself.

"#5. Manage Your Time"

Have you ever thought to yourself, *"There aren't enough hours in a day?"* I know I definitely have. But is that really a fair statement? Are you really *that* short on time or are you mismanaging your time? How many times have you checked your email today? How much time have you spent on Facebook, YouTube or Google? When you calculate the time you spend on the Internet, chatting with friends, chasing your child around or "quickly" running to the store, the hours can really add up. Of course, as soon as you make the decision to achieve your goals and fulfill your dreams, your schedule suddenly becomes an overwhelming, hot mess. All of a sudden you have ten thousand commitments and you're staying up way past your bedtime trying to get things done. The result is a very burnt-out you who is probably rocking some serious bags under your eyes. That's no way to live. Nope, not by a long shot. What you need to do is create a budget for your time. Allocate every minute of your day and write it down. Make a schedule and stick to it.

These suggestions may sound very common sense to you but the number of my clients who logically know this will work and yet don't implement this system always amazes me. Is this you? Do you *know* you should be keeping a schedule but just haven't gotten around to it? Are you the type of person who takes the time to make a schedule, write it down and then **Without time we can do nothing.** never follow it? Whichever category you fall into, know that you have some changing to do because successful people know that time is the most valuable resource we have. *"Without time we can do nothing."*

There is a third category. There are some of you who legitimately have less time than you need. I know people like you. At times, I've been you so I know the solution. Are you ready? The solution is to delegate! Delegate, delegate, delegate. Ask for help. Reach out to your support system and see who can give you a helping hand. We have already discussed how having a support system, aka your F.I.R.E. team, is important to your success. So take advantage. Well, don't take *advantage*, but definitely lean on your team or consider hiring someone to help you out temporarily or on a case-by-case basis.

I have a friend who recently told me she legitimately had no time and there was absolutely nothing she could delegate. I suspected she could probably delegate at least one item on her list and I told her so. But during that initial conversation she stood by her statement and insisted there was nothing she could hand off. Well, a few weeks later I spoke to this very same friend and lo and behold she had hired a housekeeper to come over every two weeks and help her out. When I asked what made her change her mind, she confessed that the initial thought of hiring a housekeeper temporarily while she finished her last semester at school made her feel inadequate. She felt as though she should have been able to handle it all. We have so many hats to wear that the idea of taking one off and handing it to someone else is like admitting you're not capable. We wear these multiple hats like a badge of honor. We kill ourselves to keep the house in perfect order, have dinner on the table, laundry folded and put away, kids shuffled around to where they need to be, fresh baked cookies for the office luncheon, and all the errands ran all before we get a chance to focus on our needs, dreams and desires. Can I get an amen? It is exhausting and it can be the stuff that kills dreams. By the way, if you're a man reading this, I'm sure you have your own host of responsibilities as well, at least that's what my husband says, so you pay attention too!

Don't get caught up trying to be a superhero. Make a list of priorities, do what you can in the time that you have and delegate where you can. Everything else is just frosting on the cake and cake is pretty damn good without frosting!

"#6. Be Nice!"

One of my favorite George Lopez sketches is the one where he talks about Eric Estrada. As a young 17-year-old kid Lopez saw Eric Estrada, a hero to him at the time, and wanted a handshake. For whatever reason Estrada refused, scarring George Lopez for life. In the sketch, George says, *"30 years later that kid may have his own HBO special on TV' and say, 'F*ck you puto!' There's your wake up call. I made it without your handshake."* My husband and I always crack up when he screams that line into the microphone because he does it with such conviction. He really means it. Eric Estrada's snuff affected him so much that it's now a part of his routine. But comedic entertainment aside, we can all learn from that sketch.

The lesson is no matter what you do or aspire to become, every single person you interact with is your client and your client needs and deserves the best possible service you can provide. *'But Rachel, I'm not in a service-based industry.'* Of course you are! Don't be deceived. Any path you pursue is lined with people who will be directly affected by and can directly affect you as you go by. You've got to be attentive and give them the respect they deserve. How you treat other people matters. It's what will get you a referral, open a door or help you land a big beak. It's also what will get you blacklisted faster than the speed of light and have someone tell you to go f* off on national television. It can make the difference between you dreaming about a life or living the dream.

"#7. Be a Good Sport"

In the game of life, there is one thing you must remember: be a good sport! Of course, as an unknown author once wrote, *"The problem with being a good sport is you have to lose to prove it."* That's no fun. No one *likes* to lose, but it happens every now and again and you've got to be prepared to lose with grace and dignity.

The Tailor Made Rules for Losing with Grace

✔ Before the game even starts, remember to play by the rules. We all want to get ahead. We all want to achieve our dreams and be wildly successful, but let's not get there by stepping on anyone on the way up.

✔ Pull it together and throw on a smile. Don't let them see you cry, sweat or crumble. You hold your head high and remind yourself how far you've come. You took the challenge. You put yourself out there and maybe it didn't work this time, but it will next time. After you've given yourself a good pep talk, go over and congratulate the winner. Be graceful, charming and genuine.

✔ Stay positive. I know you're sad, I know it hurts, but you've prepared for this. Remember in Chapter 1 we talked about preparing for disappointment? Disappointment has arrived, but you knew it was coming one day. Don't let this moment be the defining moment for you. All failures and losses are opportunities to learn. Stay positive and don't lose momentum.

Keep these seven "secrets" at the forefront of your mind and you'll be red hot, baby! Now that I've given you all the foundation you need to be a blazing success, you're ready to move onto Chapter 10 and create your perfect plan. As you're creating your perfect plan be sure to remind yourself the most important part of the plan is implementing it. What are you waiting for? Go get started!

Let's Wrap It Up

- ✔ The most successful people are those who are willing to put themselves out there and who are open to receiving both praise and criticism.

- ✔ You don't have to be complacent to be patient.

- ✔ Real, lasting success takes time, hard work, energy, dedication, commitment and perseverance.

- ✔ Without time we can do nothing.

- ✔ How you treat people can make the difference between you dreaming about a life or living a dream.

Notes:

_____
_____
_____
_____
_____
_____

The Perfect Plan

"Planning is bringing the future into the present so that you can do something about it now."
— Alan Lakein, writer

Earlier, we touched upon the idea of your life's purpose. Now it's time to put the pieces of the puzzle together and take action on everything you've learned. It's time to create your perfect plan and convert your dream into reality.

"Mission Possible"

The difference between a goal and a mission is this: A goal is a target or singular desire. A mission is comprised of many goals. Your mission, should you choose to accept it, is to create your personal mission statement. Developing a personal mission statement is an integral component to your success. Your personal mission statement will be the guiding light on the path towards your success and serve as a powerful visualization and motivational tool when the road gets bumpy. When writing it, think about your desired result. Are you looking to build a small local business, or an international empire? It's important to identify your big picture goal so you can establish a clear path.

In Chapter 8, we discussed the difference between wealth and success as well as the challenges money can sometimes present. That's not to say that desiring wealth is a bad thing. In fact, it's perfectly natural to want to be financially well-off. Therefore, it's absolutely appropriate for you to include your financial aspirations within your mission

statement if that is an element that is important to you and
your overall success.

"Anatomy of a personal mission statement"

There are many variations and ideas of what personal
mission statements should look like. The only thing your mission statement needs to be is inspiring and motivating to
you. If it gets you excited when you read it, then ya done
good!

Typically, a mission statement is three to five sentences
that include your desired outcome and your core values
– whatever is truly important to you and your success. But
since it's *your* mission statement it can be as long or short
as you like. As with most things in life, a mission statement is
a working document, meaning you can and should expect
to revise it periodically to match your values and dynamic
goals. To get an idea of what a mission statement looks like,
take a look at my first mission statement:

*My mission is to empower, encourage and motivate
others to live their best lives. By fully being present for
my clients, listening intently, reserving all judgment
and celebrating their successes, I am able to offer my
very best each and every session! My authenticity and
generosity of spirit allow me to reap financial benefits by
default.*

Now, it's your turn. Below are statements for you to fill in
the blanks as best you can. The beauty of a personal mission statement is there's no right or wrong. Just be honest
with yourself. I promise I won't be grading you on this assignment.

I feel amazing and magnificent when I...

I am not so great when I...

My core values are (list the things most important, i.e. your deepest priorities in regards to spiritual, emotional, mental aspects)...

When I'm working, my favorite things to do are (tasks you most enjoy doing your dream job)...

In my free time, I really love...

I'm pretty terrific at (don't be modest here, share all your talents)...

If success were a guarantee and money were no issue, I would (this is the dream big part)...

Money means...

My destiny is (why are you on this path, who are you doing it for, how will it end?)...

I most want to be remembered for...

Things I wish I focused more on but don't are (physical, emotional, spiritual)...

Use the answers from the questions above to develop your mission statement. I'm the first to admit – this is a challenging exercise. Probably more challenging than any of the others we've done so far. Don't beat yourself up if it takes some time to perfect. Just keep working at it until it speaks to you and resonates with your big picture. To help get you started, here are some mission statements from ladies I love. You'll notice there's no magic formula and each lady has added her own unique flavor. You just have to go with your gut and write from your heart.

My mission is to use my mind and creativity (through businesses, art, writing and leading by example), to teach and inspire personal responsibility and gratitude in others, along with the goal of becoming the best, healthiest and happiest person they can possibly be.

Stephenie Zamora of StephenieZamora.com

"To inspire one person to see beyond doubt, and begin living their dream life. One person at a time."

Loralee Hutton of LoraleeHutton.com

"My mission is to provide life-changing coaching for a Green Juicing lifestyle that results in a dynamic metamorphosis for your body, mind and spirit. I am also committed to living a passionate + nurturing life and guiding others along the path to realizing their wildest dreams doing what they love and sharing what they are good at. Green Juicing + Wildest Dreams + Passion = Successful, Vibrant, Healthy Life!"

Tina Pruitt of TinaPruitt.com

If you need some more inspiration try doing a Google search for other mission statements. Now grab a pencil (so you can erase and revise as needed) and get to work.

_____

_____

_____

_____

_____

_____

You did it! You've created your personal mission statement and now you're ready to roll. Once completed, don't tuck it away in a box and forget about it. Review it carefully each day and allow it to be a motivational tool to keep you on track. You might even want to consider printing it and posting it somewhere you'll be sure to see it on a daily basis. In fact, definitely print this and post it where you can see it or better yet, use it as your desktop wallpaper.

"Blueprint for your Dreams"

Step 1: Meditate on your mission.

You've created your personal mission statement, now you have to become one with it. It's important you spend at least 2 minutes a day reviewing and reciting your mission statement. This keeps your mission at the forefront of your brain and will excite you each and every day. It'll definitely help you get through the tough days! Bonus points if you commit it to memory.

Step 2: Prepare.

We skimmed the cusp of preparing for success in Chapter 1, and in Chapter 7 I shared the importance of planning to help you stay focused. This all goes hand in hand with the concept of preparation. *"Success is when preparation meets determination."* You should already have a pretty good idea of what you need to do to prepare for your dream, but just in case you haven't got a clue, let's talk about a few things you

"Success is when preparation meets determination."

can do to get there. Study, study, study. Study your craft, field or business. Learn everything you can. Consider this: before you could do anything in life, you first had to *learn* how to do it. You weren't running before you learned how to walk. You weren't speaking a foreign language until you studied it. The same is true for your passion. Know all the ins and outs of your dreams and set yourself apart from the pack. A Marine who worked for me once told me, *"I always want to be known as* the 'go-to' guy. So I make it a point to learn everything I can about whatever shop I work in." Even though he was junior to me, I learned a tremendous amount from him and he *was* always my 'go-to' Marine.

Become the "go-to" person in your field and you'll always be a cut above the rest.

Step 3: Execute a winning pitch.

"The Elevator Speech"

An elevator speech is your personal 30-second commercial telling your audience what you do and why you are special. This isn't an *actual* commercial, of course. It's really just you talking about how fabulous you are. And since of course, you *are* fabulous, you should be able to share that with the world – in 30 seconds or less.

Let's get you prepared to pitch by building the framework for your elevator speech. First write down your top 3 "fierce features." What makes you, your product, or service irresistible?

1. _____

2. _____

3. _____

Using your fierce features, list 2 or 3 supporting statements. For example, if you're nurse, one of your supporting statements might be: "I'm an expert at making people feel good." Actually, that was the opening line for a Navy Hospital Corpsman who recently pitched me his elevator speech at a workshop I taught. With that opening line, I wanted to know more about him and his skills as a healthcare provider. Super intriguing, don't you think? It's your turn.

1. _____

2. _____

3. _____

When you put it all together, you'll be left with a pitch that grabs your audience's attention within the first statement and has one or two supporting points to make your audience grasp what you have to offer, yet still want to know more. To end your speech, incorporate a statement or question that will prompt your audience to ask for a way to contact you. Take a look at these samples and use them as creative guides for yours.[7]

"Hi I'm Cassandra Cockrill...an evangelist for better thinking, better speaking, and better listening. I help thousands of people each year to be sure that they communicate more confidently and competently than ever before. I do it through Toastmasters. What about you, are you interested in better communication?"

"I have a calling. My name is Jane Saunders and I am a customer satisfaction representative who calls customers to insure they're satisfied. "Yes" is my favorite word. What's yours?"

---

7   http://www.expressionsofexcellence.com/sample_elevator.html

"I manage dead presidents! I am a money manager who helps people reduce their taxes (and my hands are pushing downward as I say this), and increase their savings and investment returns. How can I help you?"

Step 4: Back it up.

Once you have your elevator speech down, you must be sure to have the goods to back up the talk. Picture it: your dream is to be an Academy Award-winning actor and you happen to see Steven Spielberg grabbing a latte at your local coffee shop. You think to yourself, *this could be my big break!* Of course, since you've read the chapter on courage, you push past your fear and approach him. You rattle off your elevator speech and do your absolute best to show him he'd be a fool not to cast you in his next movie. What does Steven do? He looks at you and says, "Okay, kid, let's see what you've got." What do you do now? Did you *ever* think you'd have a chance to meet an acclaimed director who would actually give you a chance? Are you prepared for this moment? Do you have a great monologue ready to perform on cue? It may sound a bit far-fetched, but it *could* happen! Did you know that Harrison Ford wasn't the original pick for Han Solo in Star Wars? In fact, he was a carpenter on the set who was randomly asked to fill in while they were doing auditions. Spielberg liked him so much he convinced George Lucas to give Ford the role.

Moral of the story is this: be ready! Make sure you're prepared to showcase and deliver whatever it is you're selling in your elevator speech. It's also a good idea to have business cards, pens with your contact information, or some other memorable "take-away" that leaves a lasting impression. I started giving away bookmarks rather than a traditional card because not only are they a way to contact me, but it also helps build my brand as a writer. It's a mind association tool where they think Rachel, bookmark, book. Speaking of brands, let's move onto the next step.

Step 5: Develop your personal brand and own it.

Your brand is a way of demonstrating your value, credibility and unique contribution to the world. This is what will separate you from the rest of the pack, so you must do the following:

1. Create a brand you *love*. Your brand must be in alignment with your core values and big-picture goal. If it's not authentically you, it'll never work.
2. Take the time necessary to develop a solid, consistent brand development strategy.
3. Create your tag line and *own it*. Your brand is going to be a reflection of you and your services. You've got to be able to clearly define and articulate who you are, what you do and what your brand is all about.

The actual process of developing a personal brand can be complex; in fact, there are many books dedicated solely to developing a personal brand. For the purpose of creating your perfect plan, start with the three steps listed above and then do more research, or even consider hiring a personal brand development professional. I recommend Kristen Domingue of www.kristendomingue.com to help your ignite your brand.

It takes time to build a reputable and trustworthy brand, but it only takes a moment to discredit it.

A final thought on personal branding: "*It takes time to build a reputable and trustworthy brand, but it only takes a moment to discredit it.*"

Step 6: Crunch the Numbers.

You don't need to have a full-blown business plan to achieve success, but you do need a plan. When it comes to money, this is when a plan matters most. In chapter 8 we spoke about the money you'll need to fund your dream. And I know you did the exercises to help you determine how much money you'll need to make your dream a reality. But there are many other questions to consider. How much cash do you need to invest in yourself? Did you factor in the little costs like printer paper, copies, business cards, etc? Do you need a marketing budget? Do you need a publicist? Do you need to pay any registration, certification, or membership fees within your industry? How much will it take to create and maintain a website? Side note: If you are pursuing an industry where having a website is important to your overall success, shop around and be ready to invest in a good web designer. When it comes to web design, more often than not, you get what you pay for.

You may be thinking, *I'm not an entrepreneur; I don't need start up money. This doesn't apply to me.* No matter what you decide to pursue, there are costs associated. Suppose you want to be a nurse. In addition to the cost of your education, there are other incidental costs of becoming a nurse like the cost of licensing and uniforms. If you didn't do the exercises in Chapter 8, go back and do them. Trust me, this is super important!

Step 7: Market yourself endlessly. And then market yourself some more.

Being proactive in marketing is in essence, you investing in your brand. The more people who know who you are and what you do, the more opportunity you have to achieve the level of success you are seeking. A great way to go about this is to see what other people are doing in your industry successfully and then create a way to that, only *better*. Develop an innovative marketing plan and continue to think of the next best marketing method. Social networking is now a powerful part of our culture. Whether you like it or not, Facebook and Twitter are here to say, so get on board and start using these platforms to your advantage. If you don't consider yourself a particularly creative or tech savvy person, seek help! When funds are an issue, hire an intern. College students need internships to help build their resume and typically tend to be in touch with the latest and greatest technology. It's a win-win for everyone.

Here's a quick way to get your marketing plan started, but don't stop here. Continue to read up on marketing because it will make or break your success! Fill in the blanks.

1. My target market is: _____
   (Hint: If you're dream is to make partner in a law firm, your target might be the current partners. Basically, your target market is the group of people you want to wow and get to buy whatever you're selling.)

2. I will do the following to maximize social network marketing:
   _____
   _____
   _____
   _____

3. My top 3 competitors are: _____
   _____
   _____
   _____

4. I can set myself apart from my competition by: _____
   _____
   _____
   _____
   _____

5. The memorable marketing items I will develop are: __
   _____
   _____
   _____
   _____
   _____

6. The timeframe for my marketing campaign is: _____

_____

_____

_____

_____

These 6 marketing strategy points are an investment in your future and your ultimate success.

Step 8: Take Action Every Single Day

Everything you do should be done with a sense of urgency and intensity when it comes to your success. If you've made the decision to move forward, don't delay. Make it a point to do something that will get you one step closer to your dream each and every day. Don't just *say* you're going to do something, make it a point to *schedule* the action you plan to take and then *take action!* When you engage in the physical act of marking something on your calendar, you are more likely to get it done than if you just *say* you're going to do it.

Please grab your planner, smart phone, laptop or whatever other device you use to keep your agenda. If you don't use or keep a calendar, this would be a good time to put the book down and get one. Pronto! If you don't have a schedule keeper or just can't bear to tear yourself away from this book, then in the spaces below start jotting down the seven things you will do over the next seven days to get you on the path towards success.

Day 1: _____

Day 2: _____

Day 3: _____

Day 4: _____

Day 5: _____

Day 6: _____

Day 7:_____

Did I really mean for you to do something *every single day*? Yep! I sure did. Even a "day off" or weekend can still provide an opportunity for action. I personally like to take one day a week to reflect, meditate and visualize my day, week, month, year and life as a whole. It may not be action in the traditional sense of the word, but by taking this time to clearly focus my intentions, I am taking action to mentally prepare myself for being successful in executing the tasks I have for the week. So go ahead and get creative, get moving and get to action!

Step 9: Create Opportunities

Steps 8 and 9 can actually go hand in hand. While you are taking action, you'll want to ensure that you are creating opportunities. What do I mean by "creating opportunities?" I mean, find ways to consistently be at the right place at the right time. Network with others, spend time with people who share similar interests, and work to create affiliations. Treat every meeting, every greeting, every 'hello, how ya doing?' as a potential lead to an amazing opportunity. Not only will aligning yourself with like-minded individuals help fuel your drive, but it may also help open windows where doors have been shut. Use the space below to brainstorm potential opportunities. Think outside of the box, and really get creative, my friend.

_____
_____
_____
_____
_____
_____

Step 10: Generosity Factor

Finally, implement the generosity factor. I firmly believe that "*the most successful people give generously of their time and talent without expectation.*" Without expecting anything in return, give unto others. It's just a good rule in life. Some people call it karma, some people call it the law of attraction, whatever you want to call it, it's a nice way to live. Pay it forward as often as you can. The very easy exercise for this step is to ask yourself, "Where can I give of my time and talent?" Then go out and give!

the most successful people give generously of their time and talent without expectation.

Let's Wrap It Up

- ✔ Create a mission statement that reflects your core values.

- ✔ Creating an elevator speech can be a bit intimidating, so here are a few dos and don'ts for coming up with your kick-butt elevator speech:
    - *Don't* waste precious words on the usual clichés. **Ex: *Hi I'm Jane Smith and I'm a consultant.***
    - *Don't* bother sharing your educational information. Your audience wants concrete proof of what you can do, not where you went to school.
    - *Do* include a catchy hook that makes it conversational. **Ex: *I help women feel beautiful.***
    - *Do* focus on what makes you unique. **Ex: *My practice is the only one offering one-on-one customization.***
    - *Do* practice, practice, practice. – The way you practice is the way you perform and your elevator speech should flow off your tongue effortlessly.

- ✔ Give generously of your time and talents.

Notes:

_____
_____
_____
_____
_____
_____

❧

A Few Good People Full of C.R.A.P.

"If you want to be successful, it's just this simple. Know what you are doing. Love what you are doing. And believe in what you are doing."

– Will Rogers

"Success Stories"

One of the best ways to achieve magnificent success (with as little collateral damage as possible) is to listen to advice from people who have already been there and done that. So I thought to myself, *'Hmm, maybe I should try and interview some people from every walk of life and ask them how they did it.'* And that's what I did. I reached out to people, some who knew me and some who didn't, and candidly asked if they'd be willing to let me interview them. Some said no thanks, but the coolest people said yes! They took a chance on a new author and these are their stories. (Asking the people I didn't know personally for interviews was an extremely scary process. I was afraid they'd reject me, and of course some did, but I'm glad I pushed past my fear and am able to share these beautiful and encouraging stories. Pushing past the fear was definitely worth it!)

Fabio Viviani, Chef/Restauranteur/Reality TV Personality

In October of 2005, Fabio Viviani, owner of multiple restaurants and clubs, left his native home of Florence, Italy for America in hopes of starting over as a chef. In February 2007, less than 2 years after arriving to the new country he opened his own restaurant in Moorpark, California. In 2009, he won the hearts of millions of Americans on the hit reality TV show Top Chef Season 6. Viviani made it to the final four, but was ultimately eliminated. Not deterred by his loss, Fabio was able to capitalize on his newfound celebrity. He went on to author three Amazon Bestseller cookbooks and opened a second eatery, Café Firenze. In 2010, he returned to compete in Top Chef All Stars, although once again, victory eluded him. Despite not having won the title "Top Chef," Fabio Viviani has certainly won in the game of life. His courage to essentially start over in a new country and his resilience to multiple public losses demonstrate just exactly why Fabio has achieved such acclaimed success. To date, Viviani has nearly 38,000 followers on Twitter and almost 20,000 fan page '"Likes" on Facebook. Not bad for someone who moved to this country just a little over five years ago. He is authentically himself in all he does, but above all things, he continues to persevere as he works towards building his legacy. Despite his phenomenal success, which includes endorsement deals with Bertolli, Pellegrino and Santa Margherita Winery, the superstar chef has no plans of slowing down.

Fabio's Philosophy:

On Life
"My social life is in the public. My private life is and will always remain private. I really don't have much of a private life, but my professional life is what makes me very happy right now. What I'm aiming for is to build a legacy."

On Work
"I work 140 hours per week. Sometimes I work 40 hours in the first 3 days of the week. I've read every book on success and I took the same thing away from all of them; you have to work your face off. I'm not saying that's healthy, but it works for me. 8 to 5 pays the bills, 8 to 5 does not

build a legacy. You have to do more. To build a legacy takes a lot of work. I pick a legacy over currency right now because if you build a legacy, currency will come and you're going to be able to support the family you desire. In your life, you can work to be part of someone else's legacy, or build your own legacy and have everyone else be part of it. It's Fabio's world, you guys are just living in it."(Laughs)

On Courage

"The bad economy in Italy brought me to America. I was working a lot for a little bit of money and I wasn't a chef anymore because I was managing everything we had and not having fun. I decided to sell everything and start over as a chef."

On Resilience

"I've lost everything I had twice. If you really cook you're gonna get your apron dirty. If never anything happens to you, it's because really you didn't push hard enough. When you try to run really fast chances are that you're gonna slip and fall. And then you gotta get up again. Success is not measured by the fact that you never fall, success is only measured by how many times you get up after that."

On Authenticity

"I'm very honest. I stand behind my principles, no matter what I had to do. I'll never settle. I rather lose than win [by] lying or being someone else. I went to New Orleans in the finale of my show [Top Chef] but I didn't win because I did 3 straightforward Italian dishes, I stayed true to my style. I lost. Happy to lose. Now I represent 3 of the biggest brands in Italy. I love America but I'm very Italian and I cannot hide that. I am who I am. Be yourself. And always be honest. You cannot lie, it's too much work. You have to have a good memory to lie to people. I always say, 'Don't piss on my back and tell me it's raining because I am not stupid.' People are not stupid, you can fool somebody for a little bit, but then the truth comes out."

On Perseverance

"You've got to have good shoes, lots of sunscreen and ice cubes to chew on because you have to walk through hell to be successful. When I will fee,l that regardless of what I do in life, I will always be able to take care of my family, that day I will say my legacy has been built. I've been working for 2/3 of my life. Every day people tell me I'm crazy and they don't understand my lifeslyle und il's all good, I respect that. If being sane means to not leave a mark, I rather be a complete nutcase. I don't go where there is a path, I go where there is no trail and I leave one. I cannot stop. I only have one gear; go. If I stop, I freak out. I'll stop when I die."

On Success

"A goal without a plan is just a wish, so I had a plan and I worked very hard and we got some investors right away; we were good. And we opened our own place right away. After, like, several hundred employees in Italy, 6 restaurants and everything we had, I got no time for wishes. You gotta be willing to do more. If you do what you've always been doing, all you can expect is the same result. You have to extra do if you want to extra gain. I have no time for talk, I have to **do**. Stand behind my principle no matter what I had to do. Be real, because whatever you see on TV is who I am. Another thing that is fundamental that most people forget is to get up in the morning, go to bed at night and make sure you are the best that you can be in between that timeframe."

On Balance

"My professional life is what makes me very happy right now. Am I balanced right now? Absolutely not because sometimes I'm so busy I forget to eat. I work 40hrs in the first three days of the week sometimes. But I am very well organized. A good balance is all right; unfortunately building a legacy will lead you to an unbalanced life. Everybody who has a balanced life either does not have a legacy or has been working their face off, now has a legacy and is enjoying that. There is no other option."

Final Thoughts

"I always say you've got you be realistic with yourself. There is nothing wrong in passion. If you're passionate about basketball you can play anytime you want, but if you're not over 6 foot 6 it's very hard to be a professional basketball player. Now there are exceptions. But count how many exceptions there is and be realistic. Do you feel you are one of those? Then go for it. But just so you know, you're life will be a living hell until you make it. Are you ready for it?"

Fabio embodies all the elements we've been talking about in this book. From start to finish he's not holding back when he tells you prepare yourself to work your face off. He's talking to you straight from the heart when he shares with you how authenticity has led to his success. I learned so much from talking to Fabio. He drilled so many wonderful points home for me and I hope he did for you too. Let's identify some takeaways from Fabio's philosophy.

What was the one thing in Fabio's philosophy that stuck out most?

How does it affect your view on your own personal success?

Fabio said he only has "one gear, 'go.'" How can you put yourself in 'go' mode?

Want more of Fabio? Visit him over at FabioViviani. com where he generously gives his readers recipes,

videos and a great newsletter, which I personally subscribe to and love. Definitely worth checking out. Now,
if you enjoyed Fabio, hold onto your seats because next
we're going to read about a man who has been considered one of the most influential enlisted members of
America's 911 Force. I present to you the 15th Sergeant
Major of The United States Marine Corps, John L. Estrada.
In case you're not familiar with military ranks and titles,
John was the highest enlisted ranking Marine in the entire Marine Corps. During his term as Sergeant Major of
The United States Marine Corps there was no other enlisted member higher than him. Talk about being at the
head of the class, right?

John L. Estrada, 15th Sergeant Major of the United States Marine Corps and Presidential Appointee.

In 1970, a young 14-year-old boy named John L. Estrada
from the nation of Trinidad and Tobago moved to the United
States. Fond of war movies, particularly those featuring the
Marine Corps, Estrada enlisted in the United States Marine
Corps at the tender age of 17 with no other ambition than,
*"to be a Gunnery Sergeant. I felt then and I still feel today,
the Gunnery Sergeant rank was and is the best rank in the
Marine Corps."* Having surpassed his goal, Estrada con-
tinued to push forward and in 2004 became the 15th Sergeant Major of the United States Marine Corps – the highest
enlisted rank one can achieve in the Corps. Although he is
retired from the military, Estrada is far from slowing down.
He currently works for Lockheed Martin as a Senior Program
Manager, is a committee member of DACOWITS (Defense
Advisory Committee on Women In The Services) where he
and the committee members advise the US Secretary of
Defense on issues regarding equal opportunity for women
in the services, serves on the board of Operation Home-
Front and was appointed by President Barack Obama to
be a commissioner on the American Battle Monuments
Commission.

Rising to one of the most influential ranks in the United States military isn't an ordinary task. Such honor and prestige is bestowed upon only the most worthy of candidates. Here's what John had to say about his rise to the top.

John's Philosophy

On Life

"Life as I see it is very short and you should try to live it to its fullest. The only way you're going to really live it to its fullest is to treat people you come in contact with the way you would like to be treated. Enjoy and embrace the diversity that this world has. And respect and understand that not everyone is going to be like you. Everyone brings something unique into this world. That's what makes life very interesting. You can learn from everyone."

On Work

"The only goal I set for myself was to be a Gunnery Sergeant. I felt then and I still feel today, the Gunnery Sergeant rank was and is the best rank in the Marine Corps. When I became Sergeant Major a lot of the junior Marines would ask me, 'Sergeant Major, how do you become Sergeant Major?' My answer was always, 'Just do your job to the best of your ability.' There will be some jobs you will not like. Just do them to the best of your ability. Don't do it looking for recognition and rewards. You will be rewarded accordingly. And don't be afraid to learn from others."

On Courage

"Courage means standing up for something you know is right, it may not be the popular thing but it's what's right. Another element of courage is being able to admit your mistakes. I was never, ever afraid to admit my mistakes. I was never too big to apologize to someone if I had messed something up. I think when you do that people respect you quite a bit. And I was never afraid to say, 'I don't know how to do this. Can you show me how to do this?'"

On Resilience

"As I look at being resilient, it means you face some challenges that may seem to be insurmountable. It makes you feel there is no way in heck I can fix or address this. But you don't give up. You continue to look for ways to address that problem. You may have to use non-traditional ways. You have to go outside of the box and that's being resilient. You're not settling because something looks tough. You find a way."

On Authenticity

"When I became Sergeant Major of The Marine Corps it was a surprise to me and I'm sure to many others. I didn't know what in the hell a SgtMajor of the Marine Corps was supposed to do. I was struggling the first few months. What am I supposed to do? Am I supposed to be different? I reached out to one of my predecessor's who gave me the best advice. He said, 'John just continue to be who you were prior to getting your position. You got the job because of who you are.' Be true to who you are and your belief and your values."

On Perseverance

"Things will not always be good and what you have to do during those times, which is a quote I have on one of my coins from when I was a Sergeant Major is, 'Learning to persevere during adversity.' During those difficult times, you have to buckle time you have to stay the course. You have to believe in what you're trying to accomplish."

On Success

"I feel that those who have recognition on their agenda usually don't make it. If you just focus on doing your job and do it to the best of your ability, you'll eventually get there."

On Leadership vs. Management

"When we look at leadership and management style, there's a difference in the two. You can have a great manager who could be a very poor leader. You can have a great leader who turns out to be a poor manager. But rarely you find both qualities in one individual. Those individuals are the ones that really stand out. They are exceptional because they can lead and manage at the same time. My favorite is the leader. This is just John Estrada speaking. I think the leader is the most important of the two. Not taking anything away from a good manager. I think a good or great leader, if you look at all the great leaders throughout world history, they are the ones that have the uncanny ability to influence people to do the very best that they can. They will follow you blindly. They believe in you. It's all about you influencing them, you giving them the confidence, the way you speak to them, they way you treat them, the way you teach them. I think the leader is the most important of the two. Again, you inspire people to do more than they felt they ever could do. They believe in you. They trust you unequivocally. That's the difference between a leader and a manager. You can take a leader in any situation and they take a look at their people, they figure them out and they inspire those people to do certain things. It may be things the leader himself doesn't even know how to do. It may be the first time they are in that environment but they can inspire their people so the organization can be successful. You need both the manager and leader, but if I had to pick one, I'd pick the leader."

Final Thoughts

"There are a couple of things I'll leave you with that I feel contributed to my success.   #1) First of all, you treat people the way you would like to be treated. You treat them with respect, dignity and compassion. You still want to hold people accountable, but you can do so without stripping their dignity. That's the most important thing that makes for a good leader. #2) Never be afraid. #3) Do your job to the best of your ability and wonderful things will come to you."

Before leaving the Marine Corps, I was privileged to have met Sergeant Major Estrada several times because of my work at the Landstuhl Regional Medical Center working with Wounded Warriors. I always felt lucky to be able to escort him around and show him our achievements as a team, but having the honor of interviewing him for this book has been a true career highlight for me. I learned so much from our chat and I hope I've been able to appropriately capture and convey his message to you. Most successful people are leaders and innovators. They stand out from the crowd because they are able to captivate and inspire others to see and share their vision. What did you learn from John Estrada? Let's find out.

What was the one thing in John's philosophy that stuck out most?

How does it affect your view on your own personal success?

John said between a manager and a leader, he'd choose a leader. Which one are you and which one would you choose, why?

Next up we're headed to the Big Apple – New York City, where I had the chance to interview a brilliant, talented, creative artist Kristen Farrell. Not only is she amazingly talented, but she's also a super cool, down to earth chick. Speaking with her was like talking to an old friend. A super accomplished old friend, that is. Check it out.

Kristen Farrell, Designer Goldsmith

As a child, Kristen Farrell was always, "very into art." The talented painter, sculptor, fine jewelry designer, goldsmith and owner of the Kristen Farrell gallery in Soho says, "I always *knew that was, like, my whole reason for being."* Being a 4th generation jeweler, Farrell knew it was in her blood, but focused more on traditional art as she was growing up. It wasn't until her late teens that her love for jewelry design was sparked. Since then she's transformed her love of art and jewelry into an amazingly successful career. Kristen's work has been worn by several A-lister's such as Gwyneth Paltrow, Giselle, Janet Jackson, Tyra Banks, Brooke Burke, Jessica Alba and Pat Monahan. She's graced the pages of countless magazines and received the highest of accolades from Women's Wear Daily, W, Harpers Bazaar, Marie Claire and many more. Not too shabby for someone who has not yet turned 30 years old, right? Well, you ain't seen nothing yet, because this phenomenal lady is just getting started.

Kristen's Philosophy

On Life
"At 19, my parents took me to London for a 6-month apprenticeship. I ended up staying for 3 ½ years. I just knew. This was what I wanted to do. I wanted to start my company. I was the type of person that just focused everyday on my future collection because I always, at that point knew, 'I'm going to have a company, I'm going to have a place in Soho.' I just knew. I was very passionate."

On Work
"Every piece I design is designed by hand, I don't do anything on the computer. I actually don't do much on the computer but email. Every piece has a painting or a sketch. I keep my sketchbook in my safe because it's like my baby...I need to create. That's also one of the reasons I'll draw in my book. I just need to get it out. It can get frustrating because a lot of my pieces take so long, and I'm already thinking 5 pieces ahead and I'm still working on one of them. But, it's cool. You know, I get a lot of people that walk in and I have to explain, 'I don't mass-produce. I don't

want to. I never will.' It's always going to be a very intimate, hands-on procedure...

I love creating one of a kind and limited production pieces. But I also do try to work with all different budgets. I like the fact that people come to me and want that one-of-a-kind feeling and they can come and see me actually working. I want to create a company that in 50 years people are collecting my pieces. For me, this isn't work. I love doing what I do and I'm happy people love it. But I would still do it even if no one liked it."

On Courage

"The most important thing is to have **your** style. Don't see what's popular and then say 'that's my style.' Stay true to yourself as an artist. You should be strong. I've had to fight one of my business partners with what I believe because I'm such an artist and I definitely have my thought and way. But I fight where I believe. I've never done things like other people starting out. While others may have said let's cut back here and let's cut back there, I've always done it my way. With jewelry, you have no control over gold and the price of gold going up, and the price of diamonds going up all the time. But I always wanted to make the best. If you're gonna make the best, you have to use the best...My need to create what I'm doing is because I need to express it. I just <u>need</u> to do what I do."

On Resilience

"Honestly in the beginning, I spent a whole year before I launched this company just creating. So it was a really magical time for me. When I launched I realized there were so many other things that go into it. When I did, it was almost like I was a square wheel learning how to become a round wheel. It was very hard to start realizing more business aspects. Everything I learned, I learned by doing. Now I'm good, I am rolling. I feel like just because I want it to happen, I know it's gonna happen. I'm very gung-ho about it.

You have to be thinking positive, and thinking good things and it'll happen."

On Authenticity
"I've always stayed true to myself as an artist. I've always expressed myself. Even with my Kristen Farrell insignia I have a very strong aesthetic and I stay true to that aesthetic. I believe authenticity is the key to success. I would never trust other people to get my feeling, to get my essence out. When you're real to yourself people can feel that."

On Perseverance
"There's gonna be hard days and easy days. In the beginning I remember crying blood, sweat and tears into my pieces. I got so emotional with it. And the hard days are what are going to make you strong. You should be excited about what you're doing, but always continue on and don't be discouraged."

On Success
"The biggest success for me has been being in all these different locations around the world. Knowing that my jewelry is all over the world is incredible, it's mind-boggling. But I don't think about it so much because I'm always wanting the next big thing. I feel like the next big success is around the corner, and I feel like right now I'm hitting all my goals. But I'm going to be creating new goals and hitting more goals.

Also when you're first starting, it's hard to explain. Some people go a little crazy trying to promote their product. You never want to talk to someone because you think you can get something from them. You want to be true. When I talk to someone I always look them in the eyes, I'm not looking over their shoulder at the next person...

With celebrities and magazines and publicity it's a lot about keeping in contact with people. Or if you're at a party mingling...it was actually really funny the way I got into one of the large stores. I was at a hotel wearing one of my rings and this woman comes over to me and was like, 'Oh my god, that ring is amazing, who is that?' And you know you have a drink and you feel a little...I was like, "Oh, it's actually mine." She looked at me like, 'Yeah right,' you know because I look kind of young, not my age. So I was like, "Oh, it's mine, I made it." We exchanged info and two weeks later we had a meeting and that's how the collection got taken in there. You never know who you're going to meet. You just have to be a little vocal about it."

On Balance

"There are just things I don't want to do or don't have time to do because I have to get back to work on another piece. What I realized is that you can't do everything and to be able to delegate things is key."

Final Thoughts

"Sometimes I feel guilty that I do something that I'm completely in love with because so many times you talk to people who hate what they do. And I feel bad but at the same time, you can change it too. When you love what you do, it's hard to understand why people hate what they do, but you can do something about it. You can change what you do. I also want to reiterate with regards to support, I feel that as far as believing in me and encouraging me, my family has definitely been there for me. Even if it was a piece they didn't like initially, just knowing that they still believed in me is definitely something that has helped me get here. Having parents that let me pursue what I want definitely made a difference."

One thing Kristen says at the end of our interview, is that every person has the ability to make a change. While she has the support of her family, I want to remind you that if you're family isn't in the picture, that doesn't mean you won't make it. Your destiny is based on your decisions and you can choose to do anything you want right in this moment. With or without the support of your family, you *can* have the life you dream of having.

Take a few moments to reflect on Kristen's philosophy and answer the discussion questions.

What was the one thing in Kristen's philosophy that stuck out most?

How does it affect your view on your own personal success?

Kristen said, *"I just need to do what I do."* What in your life do you feel you *need* to do or else you'd feel incomplete?

Let me just tell you, I had a blast chatting with Kristen. She's fun, vibrant and passionate. She's one of those people whose energy and charisma are contagious. I love her and her work. She's just too fabulous for words. What the heck are you waiting for, my friend? Check out her gorgeous creations at kristenfarrell.com or if you live in the tri-state area go visit her amazing gallery in Soho, NY. Her style is the hotness. Yes, that's my word of the day – when it comes to jewelry, the hotness. Feel free to use it in your daily vernacular.

Okay, okay, I'll quit my joking around and get back to the interviews. Next we're talking to the phenomenal web and TV personality, bestselling author, international speaker, and award winning CEO of The Marketing Zen Group, a global digital marketing firm, Shama Kabani. This lady is rockin' hot and was just honored at the White House as one of the Top 100 Entrepreneurs under 30. If her achievements don't spell success, I don't know what does.

Shama Kabani, CEO of The Zen Marketing Group

Shama Kabani graduated from the University of Texas at Austin with a Masters degree in Organizational Communication. She began her career as a life coach but soon sold her practice. She went on to develop her full service digital marketing firm, was honored by Business Week as one of the Top 25 under 25 Entrepreneurs in North America in 2009 and authored the book *The Zen of Social Media Marketing* which was released in April 2010.

Shama's Philosophy

On Work

"I had a life coaching practice that I built up and sold very quickly. It's funny because I was 22 at the time. I really enjoyed it but I enjoyed building up the practice a lot more than working with clients. It's a certain realization when you realize you prefer one part of the business over another. I sold it to a colleague who I felt would be the right choice in taking it over. When I closed my coaching practice, I knew how to do marketing. I knew I was going to start a business consulting practice. When I emailed everyone and let them know I sold the practice and what I was going to do, immediately one gentleman replied wanting to be my first client. So I had my first client even before I had made that transition fully...

To start out, we didn't seek out any investors. I'm not a big fan of investors. I'll tell you why. The reason I'm not a big fan of investment is because when you have too much capital it almost makes it easier to spend the money. When you're on a tight budget you have to be creative. And your idea better be really good because often times when you throw a lot of money at marketing it can cover up a bad idea or a bad business model for a limited amount of time. When you don't, your idea really has to stand on the basis of the idea and the business. Which is a very foreign concept I think for a lot of people.

On Courage

"Critical to my success was being an editor and not being a perfectionist. Start with what you know and don't be afraid."

On Resilience

"There's setbacks in every business. The more common setbacks are day-to-day, the little things that happen here and there. The key is to keep going and to be consistent and continue to work on your skills.

On Authenticity

"Your greatest success lies in embracing who you are. On enhancing your God-given strengths by honing talent into skill. Even when high school students take their SAT Exams to get into college, they are told to focus on the areas they are best at. To me, authenticity is using who you are to do what you do best. You can't be everything to everyone. But, if you can find your strengths, and apply self-discipline, you can make it."

On Perseverance

"Marketing Zen didn't start out as Marketing Zen. It started out as After the Launch, which then turned to Click to Client and then our newest, latest reincarnation, which happened about a year and a half ago, has been Marketing Zen. So it's been a process and I think it's one of those things that people wait for the perfection and it never comes. Had I waited for Marketing Zen to become what it is today I would have never started because it can be so daunting, so you have to take the first step. I believed in delivering a good service and doing it in the most efficient way possible. You have to invest in what matters, but don't wait to get started."

On Success

"My parents have always encouraged me to do anything I wanted. I also enjoyed writing when I was younger. They always encouraged my writings, they were there if I ever won any awards, if I had a piece to read they were there to read it. I think that was very helpful because I didn't have any particular pressures or expectations. It was a very 'be happy, follow what you love' sort of home growing up. My husband now (my boyfriend then) was also very supportive when I was in college. It's not that you can't be successful if you don't have a good support system, I just think it makes it easier if you do.

I got very lucky with my success. If you think about it, the economy, frankly sucks. I graduated in one of the worst economies since the Great Depression. I know a lot of my peers who have been laid off for whatever reason and here I am and I've had all this success at a relatively young age. I recognize that, I'm really grateful for that and I don't take it for granted. I think for as much as hard work and patience and all that is key I think luck plays a fundamental role in the sense that it could have been anyone. In the Business Week article for example, of course 25 businesses were chosen in North America but it didn't have to be me. There are lots of other entrepreneurs doing some really great stuff. Things have happened in my life where I have felt like a godsend or just a stroke of good luck. I would be lying if I denied that."

On Balance

"I stay up late nights. I wake up early. You have to be committed to what you're doing. My family is fantastic. They really do so much for me and it makes it easy for me to do the things I want to do but it still takes a lot of time. It's not rare for me to be working at midnight. The great thing about working virtually is you can work anytime, anywhere but what people don't know is that then you end up working all the time, everywhere. But if you enjoy it, it doesn't feel like work."

Final Thoughts

"Invest in the things that matter. Good training, good people, and marketing. You need to invest in marketing and PR. These are very crucial. And listen to your clients. Allow them to show you what you're really good at and *then follow that. It can be really scary. The reason people don't niche is because they're scared they're going to say no to people. The more people you say no to, the more people that want to work with you, the better you get at what you do. So once you let go of that initial fear it works out really well."*

What was the one thing in Shama's philosophy that stuck out most?

How does it affect your view on your own personal success?

Shama said, *"You have to invest in what matters, but don't wait to get started."* What have you been waiting on to get started?

Shama certainly didn't wait for things to be perfectly aligned before she started. She just went for it – and did it with style and eloquence. In fact, everything she does has quality and value written all over it. Please make it a point to check out her site, Shama.tv, where she shares great business advice, provides valuable insight on web and social media marketing and a bunch of other cool stuff. If you're a business owner or are considering starting a business then you pop over to her other site, Marketing-Zen.com, and definitely pick up a copy of her book, *The Zen of Social Media Marketing 2nd Edition* which will be available Spring 2012.

Speaking of people who didn't wait, the next dude I want to introduce you to waits for no one. Eric Anthony Johnson is a man who has done everything on his own terms and is taking names and kicking serious tail when it comes to building his brand. You may or may not have heard of Javaboi Industries, but let me assure you, Eric is going to take this brand to the top!

Eric Anthony Johnson, Founder/Creative Director of Javaboi Industries Inc.

Eric Anthony Johnson, born and raised in Pomona, California, always dreamed of living an affluent lifestyle. He tried 'climbing the corporate ladder' but a government bail out resulted in his being laid off. Eric then created his own opportunity by using his unemployment checks to fund his company Javaboi Industries Inc. Javaboi Industries creates coffee-related novelties and gifts featuring its main global iconic character "Javaboi."

Johnson was the recipient of a $10,000 business grant from TheCashflow.com and continues to win contests on a regular basis. Most recently he was awarded a press release from bloggingprweb.com but he's not stopping there. His company is being courted by several investors and has one of the most loyal fan bases around. Always listening to his clientele, Eric frequently creates limited edition designs voted on by his followers. His drive, ambition and passion for his family and business explain why he's a true success story.

Eric's Philosophy

On Life

"I grew up wanting to be affluent and I tried climbing the corporate ladder. But I soon learned the corporate world wasn't all it was cracked up to be. While I was climbing the ladder I noticed there were some shady goings-on in corporate America. Different things held me back. There wasn't enough control. I started to realize there was no way I was going to get to my goal, which is financial freedom. Basically, freedom. I just wanted to be free to do whatever I want, whenever I wanted. I wanted control of my life. And money makes that happen. I don't care what anyone says.

I said, 'you know what. I don't have enough control over my life. So I'm going to go ahead and try to seek out other vehicles to get me to where I want to be.' I thought about it long and hard and I chose another career path."

On Work

"I would study other companies. I'd notice there were these awesome clothing lines and I wondered, "Why isn't it successful?" I would even call the owner of these clothing companies and ask why they weren't further along. I'd get mediocre answers and I'd just have to do more research. I figured out a lot of people just didn't have the business sense. A lot of people say you need to be capitalized and have financial backing. But I'll tell you what – if I'd had the financial backing a long time ago, without the education, I would have failed ten times harder. For me, it took me about 4 years to study the failures and successes alike. I got super confident. That's what drove me."

On Courage

"Courage to me is when you are scared of taking a risk based on what everyone else says but your gut feeling says do it anyway. Listening to your gut even though you are scared shitless and you still go for it full throttle."

On Resilience

"Blessings are crazy. Blessings in disguise come in the form of hard times. I worked two jobs to support my family while the mother of my children raised our kids. When my doctor said I needed to replace energy drinks with coffee, she also told me I had to quit one of my jobs. I quit one job and the other laid me off. It just so happened that she [the mother of my children] got a job right before I got laid off. We live way below our means and she's able to support us while I stay home with the children and use my unemployment checks to grow my company. I've built my company that way. I know a lot of people say, 'I don't like handouts.' But I like to say, 'This is the money I worked for when I worked two jobs.' So, my unemployment goes to the company."

On Authenticity

"If you have a dream I think you have to identify your core values and you have to make sure you're doing this because it's going to make you happy. Don't do something where you're thinking, "Oh, my mom and dad are gonna be proud of me." That's really stupid.

I really do not care about what other people think viscerally about my business. If you have a passion or a dream like I do, you'll know it, because you'll have it in your head 'This is what I'm doing through thick or thin.' When I had that feeling for Javaboi I knew 'I'm going to do this. I'm going to do whatever it takes.'"

On Perseverance

"I'm listening to Derek Hardy's book called The Compound Effect. When your family and friends tell you stuff like, 'don't do this, don't do that' it has nothing to do with what you're doing. It has everything to do with you making them feel guilty about what they're not doing. I have been asked, 'how many times are you going to keep changing your mind?' I've been on 4 or 5 different things. Now I hear, 'Oh yea I told so-and-so you're serious about what you're doing now." And it's not that I wasn't serious about what I was doing then. It's that I figured out it wasn't for me. It's not like I'm in college changing my major. It's just that you have to search by doing. You have to do something, and if it's not for you you'll know. You'll feel it in your heart. And this is for me. I'm still here. I'm making it work.

I don't care if Barack Obama and all his advisors came to me and said, 'You know this Javaboi thing isn't going to work. We've done research and bla bla bla.' I would still do it! And that's the feeling that you have to have. For me, it's because I truly believe that I'm doing something that can go far. I can be the first coffee novelty gifts related company that's global. I really, truly believe it – because there's not one out there. Yeah, I've been called a knucklehead. I've been told, 'it's a dumb idea; Amazon has coffee t-shirts.' But I love hearing that stuff. It's the fuel that keeps my fire going. I'll do whatever it takes. I'll die trying."

On Success

"I tried a couple of T-shirt companies. I studied all the gurus. Anyone you can think of, I've studied them. Right now I'm studying Zappos.com founder, Tony Shay's book and learning about core values and delivering happiness. At that time I was all about learning something first and doing later. A lot of people told me, 'Just go out and do something. Just go out and do something. Don't be having analysis paralysis. You're never going to do anything if you don't just do it.' But that's not how I operate. It may work for some people but for me I'm a very extreme person. I'm either at the bottom of the ocean or living above the heavens. I felt like, me knowing myself, I have to be fully confident in my product and myself in order to make any kind of move. That's what I did. When I got confident, I started moving.

I was researching everything online. I started Googling "cashflow" and I stumbled upon a site called TheCashflow.com. It was a group of urban entrepreneurs that helped inner city youth. You tell them your ideas and if they choose you, they provide awesome mentoring. They helped me through leaps and bounds. Basically, for me, I had already incorporated myself on unemployment. I had already gotten all my designs on unemployment. I knew I wanted to follow in the footsteps of Hello Kitty or Sanrio Inc.

I don't consider myself a clothing line. I'm a novelty gift brand but I just started with t-shirts 'cause I have so much knowledge in that area. I showed them [TheCashflow.com] all the stuff I had. They saw I was serious. I basically told them, 'It would be awesome if you guys help me, but if you don't help me, I understand. I'm still going to do what I have to do.' I got a call and I was told I had gotten into the program. It's an 8-week program where they give you distribution of funding up to $10,000 based on what you need. They go over things with you and tell you if you're making a wise decision or a poor one. You know some people get $10,000 and they buy up all products, not knowing that a big percentage of that has to go to marketing if you don't have a strong marketing foundation. So they help you with that, with deciding where it [the money] should go. But they don't want a piece of my sales, they're not asking for any shares. They are teaching me how to talk to investors. So if you need funding and are serious about what you're doing, thecashflow.com; simple as that."

On Balance

"4:30am – 7:00am is my time. 7:00am – 9:00pm, my kids need their father. 9:00pm – 1:00am is my time. Balance is not a myth, but it is your choice to be off balance or on balance. I have to be disciplined when it comes to what I do with "my time" which is about 7 hours of the day. Sometimes, I choose to sleep, but most times I don't. I guess I am just used to it. Honestly my morning schedule never varies. My nights do quite often. If I choose to do things without order I expect to have disastrous results."

Final Thoughts

"I think passion and creativity and education and action are my ingredients for success because one person told me awhile back my biggest asset is my drive combined with my action. I hate when people come to me with an idea for this or that. There's a lot of people working at Kinko's with ideas but don't act on it. Everyone says the same thing but it's true. You have to act on it. A lot of people say it's hard but it's not, it's a labor *of love when you're doing something you're passionate about."*

What was the one thing in Eric's philosophy that inspired you most?

How does it affect your view on your own personal success?

Eric said, *"I'll do whatever it takes. I'll die trying."* What in your life do you feel you must do whatever it takes or die trying to achieve?

Eric is relentless in his pursuit of success. The man barely sleeps yet still manages to run a tight ship at home caring for 3 children under the age of 5 while simultaneously building his business and connecting with his fans. I am always impressed at the level of productivity he generates on a daily basis. Equally impressive are his latest designs, which you can find over at www.javaboiindustries.com or keyword search Javaboi on Facebook. Keep your eyes on him – because he's about to blow up!

And to continue with explosive business builders, our next featured success story is of a young woman who is exploding in the fitness industry, my dear friend, the business powerhouse, Tarah Carr.

Tarah Carr, 1 Star Diamond Coach, BeachBody®

In less than a year Tarah Carr went from an overweight, unknown, military wife and mother of 2, to a fitness maven and business mogul. While it takes most people months to lose just 10 or 15 lbs, Tarah's hard work and dedication helped her lose 49lbs and 31.5 inches in an astonishing 90 days. Talk about a transformation! Tarah credits her weight loss success to using the BeachBody® workout program, TurboFire®, and drinking the Shakeology® supplement. As a result of her weight loss achievements, Tarah was selected as a Million-Dollar BeachBody® Finalist and though she didn't win the grand cash prize, she's certainly won in the game of life. In April 2011, Tarah officially became a BeachBody® Coach, is the leader of Team Supernatural and has been recognized on the Team BeachBody® National Coach Call as one of the fastest growing young coaches within the company, having personally signed on 78 new coaches in just a few short months. This determined 24 year-old is on the success fast track and is transforming lives along the way. Her enthusiasm, excitement and passion for fitness and business are contagious. Every time I speak with Tarah, I am left feeling inspired, and I hope her insights do the same for you.

On Life

"I never thought in a million dreams I would be the girl to help someone loose weight. I was always the seeker looking for the next best thing that was quick, easy and required little to no effort on my part. When I saw the true earning potential in my business I defined my deeper "why." I wanted to retire my husband, who is deployed 10 months out of the year. I wanted him to see our boys grow up and I realized I held the power to do so! Once I saw that clear vision, I set goals, deadlines and priorities for my life!"

On Work

"When I first became a Team BeachBody® coach, I had no rhyme or reason to what I did. All I knew was I was doing nothing different in my day besides sharing my fitness life with others – only this time, I had a website. It was not until my very first paycheck, which was $119.78. The company pays weekly so this shocked me! My Shakeology® (meal replacement shake) was already paid for! The next week, $297.87, the week after $394.61. Oh snap! Now I was making a profit! As my weekly profit grew, so did my responsibility, organization and determination to grow on the business side. My plan was to become successful in helping people and I was doing exactly that."

On Courage

"It takes courage to build a business and change lives, but the reward is beyond a pat on the back. It inspires others to show them what can be done! Be that inspiration, be you and don't forget to stop along the way to reflect on the success you have created!"

On Resilience

"I always encounter rejection. I used to get offended and would take it personally. I stopped looking at it as sales and realized they were not telling ME no, they were telling themselves no. I am always going to be around. Within time, if they still need weight loss help, they will know who to turn to. I continue to be me and help those who are ready to commit. If it's a financial issue, I share with them how they can earn back their money as a coach. I've learned to give and take a little tough love."

On Authenticity

"The biggest key in my business is coming up with unique ideas that are my own. Authenticity is key, never be anyone but you."

On Perseverance

"My biggest struggle with my business is duplicating the effort I put in to further excel. I can't make other coaches want the success; they have to want it themselves. It's difficult at times to get them to put in the work for that success. I have learned to have patience. Never give up on someone. All people achieve success at different rates. It is during these times that you must remember why you wanted it in the first place."

On Success

"The three key things that make me successful in my business are being a product of the product. Every day I drink my Shakeology®, every day I work out and every day

I post something encouraging on Facebook. The second thing I do is, I grow my team and help 2 new coaches a day on growing themselves through personal development. I match their efforts. I paint my own masterpiece!"

On Balance

"A balanced life is key, no two people will have the same balance though. I'm a mother of 2 children under the age of 4, a military wife where my husband is deployed 10 months out of the year; I live overseas in Japan and travel stateside for trips I earn with my company. My balance may seem hectic to some, but without a "to-do" list, priorities and Chalene Johnson as my influence, my life would be in crumbles. Find that person who inspires you and take notes from them. Make no excuses!"

Final Thoughts

"My advice to anyone, in any business is to never give up. Believe you can achieve anything. You have one shot at life. This is not a practice round; it's the real deal. Either you decide to go all out or sit on the sideline and watch others do it. People often wait for the perfect moment, the time when all the pieces of the puzzle fall perfectly into place. Begin any goal of yours with the end in mind. Don't wait for this and that to happen before you get started. The problem is that the perfect moment never comes, make that moment right now. There's no time to mess around."

What was the one thing in Tarah's philosophy that stuck out most?

How does it affect your view on your own personal success?

Tarah said, *"There's no time to mess around."* How are you going to stop messing around and get moving into action?

Tarah is definitely a motivated, dedicated, and ambitious young woman with a real passion for helping others. I can tell you firsthand, she has an uncanny ability to make others feel super welcomed and ridiculously motivated to take on the world. If you want to get in touch with Tarah visit her over at www.team-supernatural.com.

Last but certainly not least! To bring us home, I'm so pleased to share with you the final interview, granted to us by a woman I greatly admire and respect, my mentor Marie Forleo. Throughout this book I've mentioned Marie a few times and with excellent reason. She is nothing short of amazing. This chick **has got** the moves like Jagger! She is ridiculously brilliant and when it comes to business and marketing, Marie is among the best in her field.

Marie Forleo, CEO of Marie Forleo International, Inc.

Marie Forleo is a marketing and lifestyle expert who teaches women entrepreneurs to live Rich, Happy & Hot. She reaches over 40,000 women with her weekly videos, and leads dynamic training programs that teach women how to use hustle, heart and their desire to make a difference to live rich in every sense of the word. Her bestselling book, *Make Every Man Want You: How To Be So Irresistible You'll Barely Keep From Dating Yourself* is published in eleven languages. Marie was recently interviewed by Tony Robbins for his DVD program *The New Money Masters* and mentored young business owners at Richard Branson's Center of Entrepreneurship in South Africa.

Oh by the way, you might notice I've left this interview in the question and answer format of which the interview was conducted. Honestly, it just seemed like a better way to tell this particular story.

How do you feel you've been able to embrace the four traits of courage, resilience, authenticity and perseverance as you've built the business of your dreams?

"When people told me I was "too young" to be a life coach at 23, I ignored them and launched my first profitable coaching business. I used the Internet to downplay my age and focused on delivering high quality service and customer care.

When people told me I was "too old" to start dancing hip-hop professionally at 25, I got to work and booked a job as a lead choreographer + producer for an MTV show (this is with zero professional dance training), and I went on to become one of the world's first Nike Elite Dance Athletes with four top-selling dance fitness DVDs by the time I was 29.

In that same period, I wrote and published an ebook called *Make Every Man Want You: How To Be So Irresistible That You'll Barely Keep From Dating Yourself*, that evolved into a self-published book which sold 8,000 copies within 18 months with no major media or advertising, and then inked a traditional publishing deal with McGraw-Hill. Now the book is in 11 languages worldwide.

I've been able to successfully blend my Jersey style straight-talk and hustle with my love of hip-hop, dance, online marketing and personal development into a global business brand. Rich Happy & Hot educates over 50,000 individuals, in 108 countries around the world through our free marketing + business training content on MarieForleo.com.

I was the only female online marketing and lifestyle expert interviewed for Tony Robbins' newest training program, *The New Money Masters*.

Most traditional business advice is about focusing down on one thing. Not all entrepreneurs are built that way. Some of us are multi-passionate. We need room to explore our many talents before we settle in, or fuse them, to unleash something innovative into the marketplace.

Breaking away from conventional models in my early twenties allowed me to create a highly profitable business with nothing more than passion, my laptop, and a single belief: that every person can bust through her own glass ceiling and use modern tools of entrepreneurship to custom tailor the life of her dreams."

Was there ever a time you thought about quitting? If so, what kept you going?

"What always kept me going was that I had responsibilities - bills to pay and people who were depending on me to show up and kick ass."

When you first launched your business, did you have a plan or did things just happen organically?

"After gigs on Wall Street, and in both the editorial and advertising side of magazine publishing, I kept having this nagging feeling that I was not doing what I was meant to be doing in the world.

Though each job gave me the potential for success in terms of money and prestige, I did not want to become my bosses. For a while, I thought there was something seriously wrong with me because I kept quitting every job I had. But it finally hit me that I was meant to start my own business and make an impact in the world in my own unique way.

My journey as an entrepreneur has had many evolutions since. I started my current business for three reasons:

There's a huge gap in the market for modern online marketing and business training that's both hard-core effective and hard-core fun.

I believe the world will fundamentally change the more women become economically empowered. When women live rich (in every sense of the word - financially, emotionally, physically and spiritually) everyone wins: you win, your family wins, your community wins, and the whole world wins. I want to help make that shift happen.

Many female small business owners have a negative association with marketing. They see it as slimy, non-ethical, aggressive or pushy. This mindset keeps women earning less and struggling.

I see marketing not only as a vital skill for small business success, but more importantly as a vehicle to create art, connect deeply with and serve others, and to make the world a better place.

I want to change how small business owners, and women in particular, think of and feel about marketing. It not only helps women get the results they want, but marketing brings out our best human attributes: true listening, compassion, honesty and a spirit of service."

Have you encountered rejection and how have you handled it?

"Of course! My practice is to feel it, be honest about it with my team and close friends and move on."

What has been your biggest struggle as you've climbed the proverbial 'ladder of success' and how did you overcome it?

"To be really honest, there wasn't just one struggle. It's always a bunch of little struggles that for me, just always need to be reframed as opportunities for learning and growth. The moment I see them that way, the struggle disappears."

What were the 3 things you did that you feel have made you as successful as you are?
"I lead with my heart.
I take risks.
I'm always learning."

How do you plan to maintain the success you have achieved?

"Same as above." (Smiles)

Do you believe in a balanced life and if so, how do you stay balanced?

"I believe in a healthy life, which looks different for each person. Listening to my body, my heart and the people who love me keeps me in check."

What was your biggest fear when you first started out and how did you move past it?

"My biggest fear was that no one would "get" what I was trying to do. I actually never moved past it, I just got to work anyway."

Any final thoughts you can share with someone ready to fulfill their dreams?

"**Everything is figureout-able.** No matter what you want to create or make happen - you can figure it out, fast. Google is the world's best free research assistant and, social media allows us to connect with almost anyone in the world to help bring our ideas to life.

Always trust your intuition. Even if a deal looks great on paper, but something inside says no, trust your intuition. It never steers you wrong.

Never create a product or service "just for the money." The greatest profits (financial, spiritual, emotional) arise from where your deepest passion meets your customers' deepest need meet.

Caring is the most powerful marketing strategy there is. When you truly, deeply care about your customers, you train yourself to see life from their point of view. You articulate your customers' frustrations and aspirations better than they can. That's how you create customers for life.

No one can read your mind. You need to clearly communicate exactly what you want. When it comes to your *team and business partners: you must take responsibility for letting people know what works for you, and what doesn't. People can't give you what you want unless you tell them what that is."*

What was the one thing in Marie's interview that stuck out most?

How does it affect your view on your own personal success?

Marie said, *"No one can read your mind."* Have you ever been guilty of wanting others to read your mind and know what you want? How has that way of thinking stopped your success?

Is it any wonder I value her so much? Marie does everything with excellence and finesse. I really encourage you to visit MarieForleo.com and sign up for her weekly newsletter. Trust me, her weekly videos are **always** entertaining *and* informational. Oh and by the way, just so ya know, MarieForleo.com is a 100% virtual, women-owned and run, socially conscious company.[8] Marie is doing it up big-time, providing jobs for women and changing the world!

It was a true honor and pleasure to interview these amazing, talented and successful individuals. I have personally gained so much knowledge, inspiration and encouragement and I hope you have too. I leave you with these final words of wisdom from a visionary who built an empire out of dreams, Mr. Walt Disney:

"If you can dream it, you can do it."

---

8   Taken from the professional bio of Marie Forleo as provided by her team.

"That's All She Wrote"

Well, my friend, we've come to the end of our journey together. At least for now. I hope this book has challenged you to think bigger, dream wilder, and push harder than ever before. My vision for our work together was for you to be inspired and moved into action and for you to pursue your dreams with relentless passion at all costs. I've done my best to give you a solid foundation but it's up to you to do the real work. If you've skipped sections or half-stepped the exercises, go back and carefully read and work through them again. And of course, don't forget to pop over to my site www.thetailormadelife.com where I have lots of bonus materials waiting just for you including audio clips of the interviews.

Before you go I have one final exercise for you. Really, it's not an exercise at all. It's a challenge. Are you up for it? Here it goes. I challenge you to walk courageously, to remain resilient, to honor your authenticity, and to always remember perseverance pays. In other words, I challenge you to **stay full of C.R.A.P!**

❦

The End...aka

The Beginning of YOUR Successful Life

WANT MORE C.R.A.P?

Go to www.thetailormadelife.com and access all your FREE BONUS materials.

Worksheets

Interviews

Audios

Videos

And much, much more!

Acknowledgments

Writing this book has been a labor of love – a true test of my own personal courage, resilience, authenticity, and perseverance. But, this work was not done on my own. First and foremost, I must give all the credit and glory to God, my Creator and Savior. You have blessed me beyond measure, and I am thankful.

There were so many of you who helped encourage and motivate me throughout my book-writing journey. There isn't enough space to list you all, but please know that I am grateful for each and every one of you. Special, heartfelt thanks to the following people:

To my darling husband, Dakar Luna, for your unconditional love, support and many hours spent keeping the kids entertained while I worked. Thank you for being my soul mate, my partner, and my best friend. There are not enough words in any language to fully convey what you and our life together mean to me. You are my eternal love.

To my mother, Carmen Santini, thank you for always supporting my dreams.

To Katey Coffing, my writing coach, thank you for getting me started on the right path. I never would have made it past Chapter 1 without you.

To Diana Long, my LS, you have and always will be my anchor. You were instrumental in making this book a reality.

To Nicole Williams, the words 'thank you' are not sufficient for all you've done for my family and I this past year. From being my soundboard to my babysitter extraordinaire, you've been my go-to gal, and I thank you!

To Jessica Carpel Kupferman, girl, where do I begin? Thank you for your editing services, the late night chats, the cover re-work, and for all around being a badass babe!

To my glam squad – Melisa Miranda Jackson, my photographer, and Elsie Jaime, my stylist – thank you both for not only making me look good, but also for being amazing friends!

To Carol Roth, for taking the time to provide such valuable feedback and for challenging me to go beyond the surface. Thank you, thank you, thank you!

To Karen Salmansohn, thank you for helping me get my venti game on, dammit! You have helped me in so many more ways than you know! Thank you again!

To Fabio Viviani, John L. Estrada, Kristen Farrell, Shama Kabani, Tarah Carr, Eric Anthony Johnson and Marie Forleo, thank you so very much for allowing me the honor and privilege of interviewing you. Your participation made this book a true success.

Finally, to you, the reader, thank you for picking up this book. You have made my dream of becoming an author come true, and I am eternally grateful.

Made in the USA
Middletown, DE
15 September 2019